Christ-Centered
Intentional
Parenting

Praise for
Christ-Centered
Intentional Parenting

Sherene has created a beautiful, thoughtful workbook to help us all remember the attributes of Christ as we parent our beloved children. This book encourages us to learn through stories and personal questions how to have better responses and understanding as we navigate raising our children.

- Michelle Kendall, author of
Creating Temple Patterns in Your Home

Christ-Centered Intentional Parenting will uplift and inspire without the guilt trip! Sherene Van Dyke masterfully keeps the focus on Jesus Christ and His attributes while sharing parenting tips that are doable and Christ-centered.

-Lani Hilton,
mother of six

This book reads like a cozy afternoon on a friend's couch where problems are discussed and solutions are found. Sherene reminds us we can start where we are and move forward focusing on Jesus Christ for the parenting answers we seek. This guided study of His attributes will change your parenting and your family!

- Kirsten Ruebush,
mother of four

Sherene has put her heart, wisdom, and life experience into this beautiful book! The only success we can have comes through Jesus Christ, and she does a wonderful job helping to break down all the different ways of using the gospel to help you through so many parenting challenges and heart-stretching experiences.

- Andrea Palmer,
co-host of *Worth of Souls Podcast*

Christ–Centered Intentional Parenting

Sherene Van Dyke

CFI
An imprint of Cedar Fort, Inc.
Springville, Utah

Paperback ISBN 13: 978-1-4621-4788-5
eBook ISBN 13: 978-1-4621-4789-2

Published by CFI, an imprint of Cedar Fort, Inc.,
2373 W. 700 S., Suite 100, Springville, UT 84663
Distributed by Cedar Fort, Inc., www.cedarfort.com

Library of Congress Cataloging Number: 2024936339

Cover design by Shawnda Craig
Cover design © 2024 Cedar Fort, Inc.
Edited and Typeset by Jamie Wood

Printed in the United States of America

10 9 8 7 6 5 4 3 2 1

Printed on acid-free paper

To my kids,
who were patient while I learned.

Contents

Introduction

Pharisees and Two-Year-Olds

I woke with a start. I must have fallen asleep. It had been a long day after a sleepless night. I was exhausted. As I looked around me, I saw nothing but chaos. There were toys littering the floor everywhere, and dirty dishes stacked high in the sink. I was wearing yesterday's clothes and baby spit-up. I smelled and felt horrible! The kids and I had been sick, and life had been hard.

My "spidey senses" started tingling, and I knew something wasn't right. Things were quiet—too quiet. Where were my two oldest? I picked up Baby Gabe, checked his mouth for unwanted items, and went to investigate. They weren't in the playroom.

"Kids, where are you?" I called to them.

Then I heard Sydney's giggling voice. "We're having a birthday party for Bear."

Sure enough, Sydney and Thory were sitting on a blanket, surrounded by stuffed animals. Some animals were sporting black mustaches inexpertly painted on their faces with what looked like my black mascara. Thory was also sporting quite the "stache." Apparently Bear had aged, as had some other attendees.

Sydney and Thory were as pleased as punch with themselves. This is when I noticed the orange fruit punch in their cups and the spills seeping through their picnic blanket onto the new week-old carpet.

How could I be mad, right? It was Bear's birthday! The question I had was, would I laugh or cry about this latest creative use of items they shouldn't use? I opted for a laugh-cry. That's the best I could do. I knew someday I'd probably laugh about this, but it wasn't today!

This is parenthood; where showers and sleeping seem to be optional, and using mascara for mustaches is a good idea! We struggle and feel like we are in over our heads, and our kids seem to know it. Parenting is where we sometimes serve tears for breakfast when we can't figure out why our three-year-old is crying at the breakfast table. (Let me see, is it because I didn't have chocolate chips for her pancakes or because her imaginary friend was mean to her again? Was it my tone of voice? What was it this time?)

Luckily, there are great carpet cleaners that get fruit punch out of week-old carpet. (*Stain Extinguisher* from The Home Depot works wonders!) There are birthdays for Bears to celebrate and senses of humor to find. (I sometimes misplace mine, especially when I'm sick.) Parenting has its ups and downs! If you are tired of serving tears for breakfast and ready to try something new, this workbook may be for you.

Christ-Centered Intentional Parenting is an attribute study that links the Savior's example to parenting. Each chapter gives you a glimpse into one of His characteristics. We'll look at how the Savior interacted with men, women, and children as He walked the dusty roads on this earth. His earthly ministry can guide us in communicating with argumentative teens and tweens. Jesus stayed calm when Pharisees and scribes acted more like two-year-olds throwing tantrums than grown men. His example can influence how we raise our children.

Many of our greatest joys and deepest hurts come from being a part of a family. Some family situations are far from ideal. With God's help, we can experience more joy and heal from the hurts we encounter. Heavenly Father knew that living in families gives us the best chance of survival. He loves us and wants us to survive and thrive here on earth; to return to Him well and whole, eventually. He also knows living together is challenging, overwhelming, and incredibly hard. Jesus will meet us where we are and help us as we reach out to Him. Some days are just going to be tough, but He can make our burdens lighter. Each of our parenting journeys will look different, but our source of comfort, peace, and direction can be the same.

Matthew 11:28 reads, "Come unto me, all ye that labour and are heavy laden, and I will give you rest." Jesus makes this bold yet humble claim that can change our lives. He challenges us to learn of Him and listen to His words so our burdens may be light. He invites all to come unto Him. Why should we do this? Will learning of Him make our burdens lighter?

Looking to Jesus Christ can help us with even the toughest challenges we face in our families. He exemplified the love our Father in Heaven has for us. Striving to follow Jesus Christ brings peace. Studying His attributes can help us handle difficult situations in more Christlike, loving ways. His love will sustain us, and His example will show us the way. When we look to Him and learn of Him, our burdens will be lighter, our joy will increase, and those around us can feel His love through us. Walk the dusty roads with Jesus, and see how He interacted with others. In knowing Him, we can strive to be like Him.

His example is changing me. I am a flawed mother of five, but not hopelessly flawed because of Jesus Christ. This book is my attempt to show gratitude to Him. When my husband and I became parents, we were students at Utah State University and clueless. Well, I was clueless and overwhelmed. Kerry seemed to be a natural with our children. We had wonderful bishops who knew they had a congregation full of new parents and so they took every opportunity to teach us the ins and outs of parenting. (Dr. Glenn Latham and Dr. Richard Young were both parenting experts.) I still felt unprepared for this new role.

Being a student, I was sure I'd find the answers in books, so I read every parenting book I could get my hands on. Reading books gave me some peace of mind. I learned children are resilient and need boundaries, and that they clean up nicely when they decide to cover themselves from head to toe with mud. (I learned the latter from experience, not from a book. Just wanted to clarify.)

Bishop Young said something that changed my parenting strategy and my life. He said, "The question, 'What would Jesus do?' is the question we should ask ourselves when we face challenges, especially parenting challenges." This statement gave me hope and guidance for the next thirty years. When we humbly ask ourselves what Jesus would do, things change. Hearts, lives, situations . . . everything.

I am still learning new things, and helping others as I teach parenting classes in the wards, stakes, and communities I've lived in. Teaching these classes helped me connect the attributes of the Savior to good parenting practices. This led me to create *Christ-Centered Intentional Parenting*.

I know you are weary and overburdened, but He is here to help. This workbook is called *Christ-Centered Intentional Parenting* because it is centered on Jesus Christ. It gives parents a place to be intentional about applying His attributes to being a parent. If you let it, the example of Jesus Christ can change how you parent your children or at least enrich it. But fair warning, it may humble you as it has me. It is not easy to look to Him in all things, especially parenting. Jesus likes change, and the thing that might need changing is you and me. I know we'd like to believe that it is our children who need to change, but the truth is we are only truly in charge of ourselves. Don't worry. Jesus is a gentle teacher and will meet us where we are.

Has this piqued your interest? You may still doubt my words because I have not met your teen, your two-year-old, or your twenty-six-year-old. The open-ended nature of this workbook allows you to apply Christ's teachings and example to your children, whatever their age. I may not know your children, but you do, and God does. Focusing on Christ helps bring His spirit into our lives. It helps us overcome our mistakes and weaknesses. His spirit changes us. We see things as they are and learn to judge others and ourselves in a more charitable and accurate light. When we focus on Jesus Christ, our lives change.

We may not know each other (yet) and I don't know if you are just starting your parenting journey or whether you have been on this bumpy road for a while. The open-ended nature of this workbook puts you in the driver's seat and gives you a guide along the way. Some may feel the need to look back with a critical eye on their parenting journey. I caution you about doing this. (The rearview mirror is small for a reason!) Instead, I want you to practice saying and believing, "I did the best I could with what I knew." You'll do yourself a disservice if you say, "If only I had done this differently, if only I had known this sooner, etc." Focus on the positive path in front of you instead of looking back. Tomorrow is a new day! Keep reading and breathe! You've got this! We can find the answers to our parenting questions in the attributes of Jesus Christ. He truly is the way!

Christ-Centered, Intentional Parenting is parenting centered on Jesus Christ where parents earnestly strive to follow daily in His footsteps. Parents *intentionally* act in positive, calm ways instead of reacting in anger. Mistakes are opportunities to teach rather than an excuse to punish. Parents look for ways to express love, compassion, and encouragement as they learn to rely on the gift of the Holy Ghost and the example of Jesus Christ to parent with confidence and love.

Chapter One

Loving As Jesus Loves

Changing My Focus

Things at home were spiraling out of control, and I was at a loss. Why did everyone seem to be in a bad mood? Why couldn't we be nice to each other? What could I do?

I decided to try something new. I ignored the problems my children and I were having. Instead, I concentrated on showing more love to them. When I changed my focus, amazing things started happening.

I hadn't realized that focusing on negative things made people grouchy and made our home out of balance. Looking for things to smile about made a difference. Instead of being critical of my teenagers' hair and clothes, I let them know I cared for them and was glad I was their mom. Showing my excitement when they took part in sports became the norm, instead of whining about the long drive to watch a game. Rather than complaining about what my kids didn't do around the house, I started noticing what they did do and was amazed at their willingness to help.

Training my eyes to see the good in my children took effort. At first, it was hard to admit I had a problem seeing my family clearly. It was humbling, but somewhere along the way, I realized that my focus needed to be on the good and on sharing my love for them. It amazed me what I saw.

One time, my son Gabe thought I was going to criticize him for the way he dropped his books on the couch when he came in from school. He started huffing because he assumed I was going to complain. I surprised him by saying, "Glad you're home." He laughed at his assumption, and then he hugged me and we both laughed. It gave me a chance to apologize for sounding like a broken record. I then told him I was going to do a better job of seeing the good in him. Mentioning the good things I saw in him felt wonderful. There was so much I had missed.

To be a "good" mom, I thought I had to fix everything wrong with my kids (or at least point them out), but instilling confidence in them by noticing the good and expressing love was a better approach. Things have been different since then. Looking to the Savior helped me do this. He showed love to those around Him, and so could I.

Things felt better as I realized the role love played in our home. I didn't think it was missing, but over time my focus had shifted to the things out of place, which made our family feel out of whack. When I focused on showing love, things changed. Join me in discovering the unique role that love plays in our families. Focusing on love can make such a difference.

Focusing on Love

When we think of the attributes of the Savior, love is at the top of the list. Or is it? Love is an integral characteristic of Jesus Christ it can be overlooked. Love is also an integral aspect of being a parent, but we sometimes need to reexamine it so that it can play a more dominant role in our families. We want it to be the center of all we do, but adjusting our focus is sometimes needed.

Love can end up on the back burner when other things, like the inappropriate behaviors of children, demand our attention. It can be hard to focus on the things we love about them and put into perspective the things that are harder to love. Children can sense our irritation when we lead out with our frustrations, and then they give us more things to be frustrated about because it gets our attention. The key is to lead out with love. Love motivates people to change more than fear or rewards. People will do incredible things if they feel loved. Jesus understood this and showed us the way.

A New Commandment

At the Last Supper, Jesus gave a new commandment, asking His disciples to love one another as he loved them. Having Jesus give this new commandment right before the final hours of His life is such a beautiful parting gift to those closest to Him. We share in this gift. He wanted love to be the way His followers were recognized. It was what would set them apart from other people.

Jesus knew His disciples would need each other in the coming hours, days, months, and years to endure the hardships He knew they would face. We need our families in a similar way. This new commandment gives us something more to strive for. Showing Christlike love is more than loving others as we love ourselves. Loving others as He loves us suggests a deeper love.

We can learn to be more like Him even (or especially) in our families. Joy can be found when we attempt to work towards this type of love. C. Max Caldwell said the following about the love of Jesus Christ, "Jesus's love was inseparably connected to and resulted from his life of serving, sacrificing, and giving on behalf of others. We cannot develop Christlike love except by practicing the process prescribed by the Master."[01]

We don't have a finite amount of love to share. Love isn't wasted. Love increases the more we learn to share it. We don't have to save our love for the strangers we meet on the road to Jericho. This road goes straight through our own living rooms. Love begins at home.

Before we start down the road of learning to love as the Savior loves, please keep in mind the following quote: "None of us are perfect. Sometimes we get stuck. We get distracted or discouraged. We stumble. But if we look to Jesus Christ with a repentant heart, He will lift us up, cleanse us from sin, forgive us, and heal our hearts. He is patient and kind; His redeeming love never ends and never fails."[02] He is all these things and will help us where we are. He is truly a loving, kind God.

The Savior served and sacrificed during His mortal ministry. We can look to Him to know how to love others, especially our children. Love was at the heart of all He did. What better place to practice Christlike love than with our families? We serve, sacrifice, and give on their behalf, and by doing this, we can begin to understand charity. Charity helps us to follow in His footsteps and become more like Him. His love will guide our steps, and our love for Him will give us the strength to be more like Him. His love can be seen in many instances. Let's focus on how Jesus treated children.

Christ with Children

We are given glimpses of Jesus's interactions with children in the scriptures and from them we learn children were very important to Him (Mark 10:13-16). His love for them was evident in how He treated them. His willingness to have them come to Him when others would send them away helps us to know of His love for these little ones. The apostles were humbled by His loving act when they were asked to let the children come to Christ. They may have seen children as a distraction from the important work Jesus was doing, but the

---

01   Max C. Caldwell, "Love of Christ," *Ensign*, November 1991.
02   Kim B. Clark, "Look unto Jesus Christ," *Ensign*, May 2019.

Savior saw it differently. He welcomed all who wanted to come to Him. The Savior shows us how to love His precious little ones.

I often wondered what message my kids were getting from me. Did they know I wanted to be with them? I was pondering this during a walk with a group of women who had been around the parenting block a few times. Their insights were so helpful, and so I often asked them questions. I asked them how they sent their children the message they wanted to be with their kids.

One of them said, "I gave them my time and my smiles, especially on our busiest days. On these days, I learned to play or work with my kids first, and then I could get other things done that I needed to." Her answer surprised me. I thought her reasoning was backwards. I could see giving my undivided attention on our "normal days," but it didn't make sense to do this on busy days. Then I realized that if children's needs were met, they would be more content and less needy.

I tried it this way the next time I needed to get a lot done. I played with my kids and enjoyed being with them, and when I could see that they were playing or working well with each other, I would get a few things done. Then, when I sensed they needed my attention again, I repeated the same thing or involved them in what I was doing.

My walking friends also suggested communicating more on these busy days instead of less, especially if we were not sticking to our normal routine. Children sense something is off and it can throw them off. If they are included in the changes and made to feel a part of them, they will do better.

For instance, if they contribute to getting the family out the door for an activity, they are less likely to whine about the changes. Have them fill up the water bottles or find a missing shoe. We don't have to do everything. Our kids like to feel needed. They love "helping" us.

It amazed me how happy all of us were and the amount we could accomplish on our busy days. Sending my kids the message that I wanted to be with them wasn't as hard as I thought.

Jesus Blessed Them One by One

Imagine Jesus lovingly taking a child in His arms and calling them by name. Imagine Him smiling softly as He listens to them. It is easy to believe a child treated like this would feel His love and want to be with Him. Now picture yourself doing these same things with your children. Smile, call them by name, attach positive statements to their name, remind them of their divine worth, and take the time to listen to them. We can be His hands. We can help our children feel valued, understood, and loved. We can bless them one by one as He did.

Jesus Meets Us Where We Are

Jesus met parents and children where they were on the road. He loved all of them and wanted to be with them even if He was tired. We can be like Jesus as we try to understand where our children are coming from, the pressures they are under, and the burdens they carry. We don't have to say much. We can let them do the talking. Most of the time, we don't need to worry about saying the right thing. We just need to help our children feel heard and understood. Think of a time when you've done this. It probably wasn't difficult, and didn't take very long or cost anything, and yet it may have eased burdens and helped someone feel loved and understood.

We can watch the Savior and learn how to be more loving. His example can help us know how to show more love to our family members. Children can learn of His love through us. We can strive to share this love with our little ones, regardless of whether they are still little. Love, Christlike love, can be our number one motivator.

Love Was at the Heart of All He Did

We can put love at the center of all the other attributes of Jesus Christ because He lovingly showed us how to be each of these things. He is lovingly forgiving, lovingly calm, and lovingly patient. Love is at the heart of all He does. His love is endless. Jesus learned to love from watching His Father, and we can learn from watching Jesus Christ.

When we gain new insight into this love, it influences how we parent and bless our lives and the lives of our children. Wonderful things happen when we lead out with love. Here is an example of a mom leading out with love:

> My kids were running late to school, and I was yelling. . . again. They were crying and whining and refusing to get their shoes on. I realized I didn't want this to be our morning routine, so something needed to change. I made a deal with them. If they got totally ready by 7:10, we could play with trains for five minutes. Eventually, this became our favorite part of the morning. We made up a silly game where I had to pretend to be stressed out about fixing the tracks before the train made it to the broken part. This never failed to send them into fits of giggles. They were happy to have my full attention, and I was delighted to start my morning with

laughter instead of a stressed effort to find shoes. Five minutes of love and attention changed the course of our whole day.
- Sydney B., Huntsville, Alabama, USA

With a little thought and effort, Sydney was able to turn things around in her family. She loved her children, but was concentrating so hard on the problems that she was making things worse. If our focus is always on the problems, we are likely to have more problems. If our focus is on showing love, our children are more likely to feel this and less likely to misbehave. Taking a step back and training our eyes to see the good can give us more opportunities to express love. (See chapter five for more help with this practice.) Love is an integral part of our Savior and ourselves.

Sister Bonnie H. Cordon reminds us that love is a powerful tool. She says, "The greatest tool in our 'intentional parenting toolbox' is love, the love we receive from our Father in Heaven, and generously extends to our precious children. Love is the foundational virtue of building a strong home." In this same address, Sister Joy D. Jones goes on to say, "The greatest gifts we can give our children will be the simple, but intentional daily acts of love and care inspired by the one who showers us with His perfect love."[03]

These quotes help us know where to look for examples of how to love. They cause us to think about the daily acts of love we show our family. We may wonder if our family members know we love them. Do our actions reflect this love? We can focus on the simple things we do daily that show our love, and this helps us avoid feeling overwhelmed. Loving daily acts can change the atmosphere in our homes especially when we look to Jesus Christ to show us the way. (We'll work on solving trouble spots in other chapters in this book. For now, focus on expressing love). Here is an example of something we added to our daily routine to help our home be a loving place:

Thory decided he was too old to hug me anymore. Maybe I had hugged him at the bus stop too many times. My heart ached. I knew I didn't want hugging to be a thing of the past, but I didn't know what to do.

As I prayed about this, I realized the answer was in the daily routines my husband and I had established. We could just routinely continue to give Thory and our other children hugs. If it was just a part of our day and not in front of his friends, hugging could still be something we did as a family. It was easy to add "family hug time" to our routine after reading our scriptures and prayer time. It gives all of us a chance to express the love

03   Cordon, Bonnie H., and Joy D. Jones, *Intentional Parenting*, BYU 2017 Women's Conference, Provo, Utah, May 5, 2017.

we have for each other in a non-threatening way. My sons are now twenty-five and twenty-eight and have no problem hugging their mom during "Hug Time" or any other time. They never hesitate to say, "I love you" and laugh when they accidentally say it to their friends when they say goodbye on the phone. It didn't take much to establish "Hug Time" as part of our routine. And it has made expressing love easy, for which I am grateful.

Try noticing the times you show love to your family. Then systematically add more expressions of love throughout your day. I know it sounds weird to schedule times to show love to others, but the logical side of our brain craves structure. It won't take long before this way of thinking becomes automatic. For instance, if your kids are whiny and clingy, add in some positive, loving attention earlier in your day, and then their whininess may decrease.

Things change when love is at the heart of all we do. It may be easier to express love when they are little, but we can make adjustments as they grow. Prayer and continuing to be systematic can help us be in tune with the ever-changing needs of our family. If something just feels off in our family, we can increase the Christlike expressions of love we show family members.

To see changes in our homes, we can remain positive and gentle with our attempts and the attempts of our spouses. It takes time to change. The Savior would focus on our steps forward, no matter how small. Practice being gentle as He would be. Remember that Jesus spent His whole life living these attitudes and actions. Filling our days with more of His love will take time. Pray for help and the Lord will bless you. We can move forward with faith. His example will help our hearts to be full of love.

Intentional Loving
Workbook

The Savior was intentional in the way He lived His life. He took time to reflect, ponder, and center Himself on His work. When we take time to reflect and ponder, we will act with more purpose instead of reacting to the current conditions around us.

The parenting workbook section helps us to ponder and reflect on things near and dear to our hearts. Writing things down helps to commit ideas, concepts, and sincere desires to our hearts. It also gives us a place to ponder the question, "What would Jesus do?"

Now that you have studied a few things Jesus did to show love, take time to ponder the questions below to be more intentional as a parent. It may surprise you how good it feels to know that you are trying to follow in His footsteps.

1. How did the Savior show love to others?

_____

_____

_____

_____

2. How do I show love to my family members?

_____

_____

_____

_____

3. What can I do daily to show more Christlike love to those around me?

_____

_____

_____

_____

4. How can love be the most used tool in my toolbox?

_____

_____

_____

_____

Think of specific ways you can be more intentional with the love you show your family members on a daily basis.

_____

_____

_____

_____

Loving Daily as Jesus Did

To intentionally parent in more Christlike ways, we can look closely at our daily interactions. Use the chart below to make a note of when love is expressed to family members.

1. What things do you specifically do to express love?

Example:

7 a.m. Hug children after scripture time.

10 a.m. Put down my phone and play with kids during puzzle time.

1 p.m. Show compassion and stay calm when kids whine about nap time.

Now it's your turn. What can you add to your day that expresses your love?

Morning:

Afternoon:

Evening:

2. Now, using a different color of ink, add other things that will let your family members know of your love for them.

3. Go back a third time with a new color and add some Christlike-loving things to your day.

4. Put a star by the things you want to work on this week. Put a check on the things that have now become part of your routine. Please refer back to this to remind yourself to build your foundation on love.

5. Did these things help the atmosphere in your home?

_____

_____

_____

_____

_____

_____

_____

6. Has adding these things brought peace to your heart?

_____

_____

_____

_____

_____

_____

_____

Chapter Two

Compassionate Listening

Compassion may be the most distinguishing characteristic of the Savior. His consideration for others was evident with every step He took. Jesus understood those around Him, whether they struggled from sin, sorrow, or life's challenges. He showed mercy and understanding. Jesus put the needs of others before His own and went out of His way to ease the burdens of those suffering. His ability to listen changed lives for the better and made it possible for healing to take place. Jesus continues to be generous toward all of us. His compassionate acts can inspire us to work harder to understand the needs of our loved ones. Here are two instances Jesus showed compassion.

The Widow of Nain

In the small, remote village of Nain, a widow's only son died.[04] Jesus met his burial procession just outside the village and brought this young man miraculously back from the dead. It was no coincidence that Jesus happened upon this village when He did. He knew the utterly desperate situation of this widow. He was there for her in her moment of greatest need. Nain is a thirty mile uphill walk from Capernaum, where Jesus and His followers had been the day before. Jesus and His disciples possibly walked all night to meet this burial procession just outside the city gate. What a beautiful miracle this is! It reminds us we matter to Him and He will be there for us. He will meet us where we are. Jesus steps forward and says, "Weep not."

How can we do likewise?

---

04   Luke 7:11-16

There are times when the Lord calls on us to be His hands. Easing the burdens of others is part of being a disciple of Jesus Christ. It is also a part of being a family. Some of us would rather believe we are just not a compassionate person, but we are selling ourselves short. It is a lot easier than we think. Sometimes it may mean going to great lengths to be with someone. But other times, it can be as simple as returning a smile. Sometimes it takes picking up the phone to reach out to someone, other times it's putting the phone down to pay attention to a child who needs a listening ear. Easing burdens may not be as complicated as it seems. If the Savior can walk thirty miles in the dust to ease someone's burden, we can listen to a loved one when they need to talk. Sometimes listening is all it takes.

Listening in Compassionate Ways

In one well-known bible story, Mary and Martha grieved over the death of their brother, Lazarus.[05] They were distraught. Jesus had not been there. When He came, Mary and Martha both sought comfort from Him. Jesus listened to each of them with His eyes, ears, and heart, and because He was listening in this way, Mary and Martha shared their feelings in their own ways. Martha rushed to Him and Mary stayed back. Both knew Jesus was listening. How can we let our children know we are listening and want to ease their burdens?

Here are some steps we can take to listen as He listens:

- **Show them you care**: Send the message you are listening with your eyes and whole body like the Savior did. Put down your device. Your attention alone will encourage them to talk. It sends the message that you care about them and are there to help.

- **Stay quiet so they can talk**: Jesus showed He was listening by being quiet. He let Mary and Martha talk. Then they both shared the burden of their hearts. It's hard to listen to someone if you are talking. Sometimes we think we have to do a lot of talking when someone brings a concern to us. That's just not the case. Most just need someone to listen and share their burden. It is okay to ask questions that clarify or summarize complicated stories, but remember your words are to make further space for them to share.

- **Listen for and recognize their feelings**: The Savior let Martha talk and didn't correct her thinking. Through the course of their

05   John 11:1-44

brief conversation, she fixed her thinking about the Savior's power over death. She understood Jesus could not only heal the sick, but He had power over death. When others voice their feelings, they often "fix their thinking," just like Martha did. Part of acknowledging a child's feelings is helping them name what they are feeling. Parents can say things like, "You sound hurt that your friend didn't invite you to the party. Is that right?" Naming the emotion they are feeling helps them feel understood and if you didn't attach the right emotion, they will let you know. This also helps them clarify what they are feeling or not feeling. Helping the child to understand the emotions they are feeling is a step forward in helping them to deal with these feelings. Showing empathy to a child lets them know you care and are available to listen. Just be careful that your own emotions about the event don't fuel their anger or hurt. Draw the line at feeling a portion of what they feel without adding your feelings to the mix.

• **Keep your focus on the one suffering**: Martha and Mary pointed out to Jesus that their brother would not have died if He had been there. Jesus could have taken offense because they reminded Him of this, but He didn't. His focus was on the ones suffering. We can do likewise. We can be more concerned about the feelings of others than our own need to be right. If we make a mistake, we can apologize. If they made a wrong assumption about something we did, we can correct misconceptions later. Keep them talking and working through the emotions they are feeling. (My friend, LaDawn Moon, reminds herself of the following if she feels hurt, "I can be humble and hear this. I know Jesus understands me and that is enough for right now.")

• **Give them a chance to predict consequences**: In this story, we see Jesus lead Martha to the knowledge that He has power over death. He gives both Mary and Martha a chance to predict what could happen to Lazarus. They had witnessed the miracles Jesus had performed, but were possibly afraid to hope their brother could be restored to them. They soon learned that with God, all things are possible. Lazarus rose from the dead! What a beautiful moment for this family, and for all of us. Jesus has power over death.

- **Help them recognize the truth:** People tend to create stories about what they think is going to happen, and that quickly becomes their perceived reality if they aren't kept in check. By giving people a chance to express their predictions, and then, like Mary and Martha, be brought back to truth and actual reality, we help them avoid catastrophizing and assuming the worst. It's good for people to do their own thinking, but having someone slightly removed from the situation helps individuals to come up with a plan.

- **Look for solutions together:** Helping others to come up with solutions to their problems is important. Our family members need safe places to work through things. We can be that for them. Being encouraging and saying things like, "What can you do about that?" helps them to look for solutions instead of getting stuck repeating the perceived or real problem at hand. After they tell you their ideas, help them predict the consequences of each alternative they come up with. Ask them, "What do you think would happen if you did that?" (This process will be explained further in the workbook pages of this chapter). The child or teen should come up with their own solutions, but you can make some suggestions if they get stuck. Try to send the message that you believe they can handle things, and that you will not tell them what to do. "I don't know what you will decide to do, but I know you can do this. If you still need to talk about this, I'm here."

- **Check in with them:** After the family member has handled the problem, check in with them to see how it went. Being a good listener starts all over again!

Listening Heals Hearts

Listening is a piece of the puzzle to becoming Christlike. We heal hearts when we listen. Jesus listens, and this is how He understands the needs of all of us. Christ's compassion helped Him to ease burdens. Being compassionate and listening to others helps us know how to act. Acting on our compassionate thoughts and feelings leads to healing. We will explore helping our loved ones heal in Chapter Nine. Listening is also a key to dispelling anger (Chapter Twelve) and teaching our loved ones without sounding preachy (Chapter Eleven). We'll explore these concepts later. For now, concentrate on listening. These skills build on each other, so get a good foundation and then move on.

Showing compassion by listening can be something we do every day. We shouldn't "save up" our compassionate listening for the hard moments in the lives of our loved ones. We never know when someone will open up to us and share the contents of their heart. When people know we will listen to them, they are more likely to share both the good and bad moments of their lives with us.

Find activities that help your family members open up. Things like going for a walk, washing dishes together, or skipping rocks on a river give others opportunities to open up about what is going on in their lives. Activities that help people relax also help individuals to open up.

Another time people want to talk is at the crossroads during their day. When children come home from one activity to start a new one, it is a good time to talk because they have things they want to share. When we are willing to share these small crossroads with them, they may be willing to share when larger difficulties come.

Listening gives us clues about our loved ones' concerns and that knowledge will help us be compassionate. People feel less anxious and more in control of their lives when they feel understood. When people feel understood, they feel more secure about taking on the challenges they face. Listening to their concerns and worries instills them with the courage they need to face challenges.

We might think Jesus went around telling people what to do to make their lives better. This assumption is wrong. Jesus did a lot more listening than we are aware of. Jesus listened to people, which may have set Him apart from other rabbis. Other rabbis and teachers may have felt people should listen to their wise counsel. Jesus's humble inquiries showed others He cared about them. This may have been why people confided and trusted in Him. We can be better listeners so our loved ones confide in us. Jesus showed us how to listen to the concerns of others. Listening heals hearts.

Jesus Understands the Needs of Caregivers

Jesus truly understands the weight many of us feel regarding the care we give our loved ones. Take comfort in knowing He knows what it is to put the needs of others before our own. He is aware of what we are doing and understands the burdens we carry. The following story illustrates this point:

> Recently, feeling consumed in constant care, I sought relief in the scriptures and read in Matthew the account of Christ's feeding of

the five thousand. As the scriptures unfolded, I saw how they related to mothering and I was consoled in my moment of need.

As Matthew states, during the Savior's selfless ministry, the Lord learned of the brutal death of his servant John the Baptist. Jesus left shortly thereafter by ship to 'a desert place apart.' [06] But instead of solitude, he met up with a multitude in need of his healing and care.

Moved with compassion toward them, Jesus postponed any moment of renewal he might have desired and responded to their needs. Not only did he heal their sick, but he saw to it that all present were fed. After the multitudes and his Apostles had departed, Jesus took his own leave 'up into a mountain apart.' [07]

As I read these verses, I came to feel by the Spirit how much the Savior understands my trying moments. He knows the feeling of being surrounded by people in need, of having people follow him from 'out of the cities' [08] all day and even into the night. He experienced feeling physically spent during his earthly ministry. Surely, then, the Lord empathizes with my demanding role as a mother and is keenly aware of how my children's outstretched arms and tearful eyes often delay my own restful intermissions. [09]

Thinking of the Savior's compassion can be humbling. We can be overwhelmed with the thought of striving to be like Him or take comfort that we can learn so much from His example. Striving to more completely show compassion for others is something we can do. Picturing the Savior may help us be in the right frame of mind to handle some of the challenges we face. We can picture ourselves being His hands. We can do the work of caring for someone else for Him as a way of showing our love for Him. Joy comes from this type of service. Sometimes we need to remind ourselves we are serving Him and not just making ourselves exhausted.

Jesus went out of His way to ease the burdens of others. As His disciples, we are instructed to "go and do thou likewise."[10] However, the thought of doing this may be intimidating, or even frightening to us. Let me clarify, I am not suggesting that to truly be compassionate we have to take on others' burdens completely. That is the Savior's role. There is, however, a role we can play in easing the burdens of others. Sometimes our loved ones need a

---

06   Matthew 14:13.
07   Matthew 14:23.
08   Mark 1:32-37.
09   Karen Rose Merkley, "Loaves, Fishes, and Compassion," *Ensign*, March 1995.
10   Luke 10:37.

listening ear to work through a problem, other times they need someone just to listen to how they'll solve a problem. Other times children's burdens need to be shared or taken on by a loving adult. We'll explore how to tell which role to play in Chapter Nine, but for now, concentrate on learning to listen. It is the basis for many of the attributes we'll study in this book.

Remember, compassion goes a long way with our loved ones. If people feel understood, it is easier to feel loved. And if they feel loved, they are more likely to feel safe and happy. When opportunities arise to show compassion, simply do the best you can. Listen, comfort, and share the burdens of those you love. His grace will sustain you, and His love will shine through you. He will help you to be His hands.

Compassionate Listening

Workbook

1. Choose a situation or problem at home where you could you use the Savior's example to communicate more compassionately.

_____

_____

_____

_____

2. How would the Savior show compassion in this situation?

_____

_____

_____

_____

3. Using the prompts below, write out what you could do to be a more compassionate listener in this situation. Try and see yourself being more like the Savior.

I could show them I care by:

_____

_____

_____

_____

I can stay quiet so they can talk by:

_____

_____

_____

I can choose to keep my focus on the one suffering by:

_____

_____

_____

_____

I can give them a chance to predict consequences by:

_____

_____

_____

_____

_____

I can encourage them to predict consequences and recognize truth by:

_____

_____

_____

_____

I can check in with them to see how they're doing by:

_____

_____

_____

_____

4. If you did put this exercise into practice, how did your loved one respond to your efforts?

_____

_____

_____

_____

5. What did you like about how you communicated? Did you feel your responses were more Christlike?

_____

_____

_____

_____

6. Is there anything you would do differently next time?

_____

_____

_____

_____

_____

_____

_____

_____

_____

_____

_____

_____

_____

_____

_____

_____

_____

_____

_____

Chapter Three

The Space Between

"Our prayers follow patterns and teachings of the Lord Jesus Christ. He taught us how to pray."

- President Russell M. Nelson

Have you ever wondered what a "typical" day was like for the Savior? In Mark 1:35-45, we get a glimpse of a "typical" day for Him. We see Jesus had many demands placed upon Him. He cast out devils, healed lepers, and taught in synagogues. We see instances where He was challenged on every side and had obstacles to overcome. His days were full, and yet He rose early in the morning to spend time with His Father. Praying helped Him to have the courage to do the hard things asked of Him. In this chapter, we will discuss how the Savior took time to pray, and how we can incorporate that direction in our own lives.

Mark said it this way, "And in the morning, rising up a great while before day, he went out, and departed into a solitary place, and there prayed."[11] Mark included the fact that Jesus rose up a "great while" before the day, possibly because it stood out to him and was out of the ordinary for others of that time. We see here how prayer was a big part of how Jesus prepared for the days He spent on Earth. Jesus was intentional about the time He spent with His Father. He prayed to align His will with His Father's. He wanted to invite His Father to be with Him in the work. We want this as well.

Our days may not include healing lepers or casting out devils, but there are similarities. Our days are very full and we have many demands placed upon us. Jesus had many who were seeking Him. (Does this sound

---

11   Mark 1:35.

familiar?) The demands of parenting can weigh so heavily on us. Prayer will help us meet the demands of our day.

Jesus filled His days during His Mortal and Postmortal life much like the one Mark described. "*[Jesus] went about doing good*" (Acts:10:38). He accomplished so much because His Father was with Him. Prayer connected Him to His Father. Because of this connection, Jesus responded well to the challenges He faced and stayed true to who He was. Our prayers connect us to God and help us stay true to who we are. His example of turning to His Father in prayer is a pattern we can follow. Here are a couple of things Jesus teaches us about prayer.

Jesus Modeled How to Align His Will with the Father's

We sometimes have mistaken beliefs about prayer. Prayer is not like rubbing a magic lamp with a genie that grants wishes. Heavenly Father is not here to grant wishes on demand. He's here to listen, soften our hearts, ease burdens, give comfort, help us learn, and inspire us to find solutions to problems, to name a few. When we are new to praying, our view is limited, but as we learn and grow, we come to understand how prayer can bless our lives. Developing a relationship with Heavenly Father takes time and personal change as we better understand the purpose of prayer. It's humbling to admit we can't do something on our own and need help. But when we humble ourselves, prayer can change things.

Sister Jean A. Stevens sheds some light on creating this type of relationship. She says, "We can trust that He will help us, not necessarily in the way we want, but in the way that will best help us to grow. Submitting our will to His may be difficult, but it is essential to becoming like Him and finding the peace He offers us. We can come to feel, as C. S. Lewis described: 'I pray because I can't help myself . . . I pray because the need flows out of me all the time, waking and sleeping. It doesn't change God. It changes me'" (2014).

We change when we pray. Our hearts soften when we share our burdens with God. We are not the same person after we pray and submit our will to God. Our willingness to pray allows Him to enter our story and the lives of our loved ones, but we have to be willing to invite Him in. We are not alone. He will be there for us. We can trust in Him and face our challenges with prayer. Being humble enough to align our will with His takes courage. Here is how one young mother changed her prayers and her understanding of prayer. If you watch for it, you can see when Kenna's prayers change from a "grant me my wish" kind of prayer to a prayer of a person willing to accept God's will.

> *My third child has a more difficult time sleeping through the night than my other children. In addition to him just being a light sleeper, I now realize ear infections and allergies seem to have been contributing to his sleeping problems.*
>
> *Over the last twenty months, when he happened to sleep through the night, the older two kids would wake up! During some of those extremely trying stretches I wondered, somewhat dramatically, how much longer it would take for me to just collapse from exhaustion.*
>
> *Each night I kept praying earnestly, and oftentimes desperately, for my children to sleep through the night. Over and over again, I awoke to the dark night sky with no sign of dawn, disappointed that my prayer seemed to be ignored.*
>
> *I would just walk out of the room after rocking the baby back to sleep, lie down, and hear his cries start again. "Heavenly Father," I cried out in my heart, "I know that you have the power to heal, to raise people from the dead, to cause sleep to come over a person or an entire city of Lamanites. Why can't you make my one little baby sleep? I am trying to do thy work, and it's hard enough with a good night's rest, let alone without! Can you please help me get some sleep?"*
>
> *And after some time of these increasingly frantic and repetitive pleas, I realized that I needed to change my prayer. "Please help him sleep, but if not, help me figure out what he needs. Help me get a nap tomorrow, or help me to have enough energy to take care of the kids and get my things done at work . . .*
>
> *Once I changed my prayers, I was certainly less disappointed. I could also see that the Lord was helping me with all the other things I was praying for. I learned that He doesn't always take our trials away. But He will help us through them when we change our request from "please take this away" to "but if not, help me handle it."*
>
> *- Kenna Stuart, Riverdale, Utah, USA*

"But if not," is such an important phrase for us to use in our prayers. It shows we have a humble heart and are willing to submit to our Heavenly Father and trust that He knows what is best for us. We can still ask for what we would like to be blessed with, but if He has something else in mind for us, we can say, "but if not," knowing that He loves us still. Learning to accept His will can be hard, but He will bless us when we keep our hearts soft.

Kenna's growth is humbling. Many of us have had desperate nights like she described. These long nights can be so agonizing! Kenna rose above her trials, and instead of becoming bitter, she became better. One particular sentence from her last paragraph is so enlightening: "I was certainly less disappointed." How many of us choose to be disappointed that Heavenly Father didn't answer our prayers the way we wanted when we wanted them answered?

Being willing to change our prayers and look at our situation with new eyes makes things more bearable. It also helps us to see His hand in our lives. He may not remove our trials, but He will help us through them according to His will. He looks at the potential for our overall growth and not just our short-term comfort. Kenna's prayers changed her, and our prayers can change us when we are humble enough to align our will to His.

Prayers Can Be Part of Our Parenting Solution

Jesus spent much of His life praying—should we not also do this? It was His habit to pray often. We get glimpses of this in the scriptures. Jesus prayed for comfort and to give comfort to others. He prayed when He blessed and healed others. He expressed gratitude to His Father when His heart was full of joy, and went to Heavenly Father when His heart was full of sorrow. The prayers Jesus uttered were often on behalf of others. We can turn our hearts to God through prayer throughout our day. Jesus showed us a pattern of prayer to follow. Prayer can be part of our parenting solution.

It takes courage to become a parent. Being responsible for someone else is a big challenge and something we can make a matter of prayer. When we pray for our children by name, we not only ask Heavenly Father to be a part of their lives, but our hearts also soften as we specifically pray for an individual. We are forming a partnership with God to bless this individual.

We see Jesus doing this at the end of His life when He prayed for Simon Peter (Luke 22:31-32). Jesus loved Peter and wanted what was best for him. Can you imagine what it felt like to know that Jesus prayed for you by name? The Nephites described it this way, ". . . no one can conceive of the joy which filled our souls at the time we heard [Jesus] pray for us unto the Father."[12] Prayer changed their lives and gave these Nephites something they would never forget. Christ's prayer stayed with Peter as well and helped him to have courage.

Praying for others is a powerful tool. It invites God into our story and our children's stories. Our feelings change when we consistently pray for

---

12   3 Nephi 17:17.

people by name. Our connection to them is strengthened and our interactions with them can be more in tune with God.

A few years back, I relied on prayer to get over a hurt caused by my daughter. She said something unkind, and I tried to act like it didn't bother me, but I was hurt. It wasn't until I took this hurt to the Lord in prayer that my feelings were able to change. "Heavenly Father, I was hurt today by what my daughter said. I know she didn't mean it and she apologized, but I still feel hurt. I don't want these feelings to affect our relationship. I want to forgive her. She is trying to be kinder and I sense this in her. Help me to focus on this and not on the hurt she caused me . . . " This prayer kept my heart soft and I was able to get over my feelings. I said her name as I prayed. I could feel my heart softening toward her.

When we consistently pray for people by name it changes how we feel about them. This prayer affected how I treated my daughter. I didn't lash out, or find a way to hurt her back. Involving God helped me to see her efforts and helped me to stay kind.

Our prayers can guide our footsteps and help us to have strength to do hard things. They can help us gain understanding and find direction. Prayers soften our hearts and help us to know the right words to say. They might remind us of harsh words we have spoken and help us to find a better way to communicate with loved ones. Prayers are powerful. Having a prayer in our heart throughout our busy day helps the day to go better, and helps us respond in more Christlike ways.

In Alma 37:36, it reads, "Yea, and cry unto God for all thy support; yea, let all thy doings be unto the Lord, and whithersoever thou goest let it be in the Lord; yea, let all thy thoughts be directed unto the Lord; yea, let the affections of thy heart be placed upon the Lord forever." When we have a prayer in our hearts, Elder Bednar says the following can happen, "We notice during this particular day that there are occasions where normally we would have a tendency to speak harshly, and we do not; or we might be inclined to anger, but we are not. We discern heavenly help and strength and humbly recognize answers to our prayer. Even in that moment of recognition, we offer a silent prayer of gratitude."[13] Prayer changes us and helps us to be better and more in tune with God. Prayer helps us fight off our natural man tendencies (Mosiah 3:19) and find more Christlike ways to respond.

When we counsel with Him in quiet moments, He can help us to know what to say and do during our stressful moments when things may literally be on fire. We can rely on the Lord to remind us to slow down so He can

---

13   David A. Bednar, "Pray Always," *Ensign*, October 2008.

direct our paths. When we make the effort to turn to Him, He will give us the space we need to respond.

Prayers Lengthen the Space Between a Stimulus and a Response

When we counsel with the Lord, we have God with us and this helps us to handle stressful situations including children fighting over toys or crying when they don't get their way. Or when the toast burns, and socks get lost, and this is all before eight o'clock in the morning! How are we supposed to stay calm and patient when there is so much commotion around us? How can we prepare for these ups and downs?

We have a choice in how we respond to the things that happen to us. Things come at us pretty fast, and it may seem like we have no time to think about our response, but seeing that there is a space between what happens and our response can make all the difference. Prayer lengthens this time. Instead of just reacting without thinking about what we are doing, we can pause and ask the Lord for help, which can change our response.

Prayer is often the key to responding well to the stresses of our day. Prayer in the morning helped Jesus to handle the stresses that came His way. Our prayers can help us create space between when something happens and when we respond.

For the longest time, I have looked for a way to explain what I feel when I combine praying and looking to the Savior for help in staying calm in stressful situations. It is almost as if time slows down, and I am able to think through how I want to respond instead of reacting negatively or angrily. It feels like the things around you slow down or are moving in slow motion. It is an amazing thing to experience.

Let me walk you through this. A stimulus is what psychologists like B. F. Skinner call an object or event that elicits a response. The scriptures call these objects or events "enticements," and we are given an opportunity to choose how we will respond to these enticements.

Today, the buzzword is "triggers." You can choose what to call them. We'll mostly use the word "trigger" because, to me, a trigger is anything that irritates us and could cause us to respond in an angry, combative, or harsh way. We may feel we have no choice in how we respond, but the opposite is true.

It is explained this way in Stephen R. Covey's book, Living the 7 Habits, "Between stimulus and response there is a space. In that space lies our freedom and power to choose our response. In our response lies our growth and our happiness." [14] We choose how we will respond to the situations that arise in our lives. Our power to choose our response gives us freedom to act or be acted upon.

Prayer can be that pause between stimulus and response. It won't be a long prayer or even a formal prayer, but just the act of calling upon God for aid can help us slow down to avoid just reacting to stimuli. If you are a visual person, picturing the Savior before you respond to something stressful can be calming. If you have a favorite picture of Him that is easy to recall, picture that specific image of Him. Picturing Him slows things down, and if we've been prayerful throughout our day, we are more likely to stay calm (most of the time).

But this can be hard! We often react without thinking. Somebody does or says something to us and we react. We frequently don't choose our behaviors because we are too busy just reacting to what is coming our way. It's reflexive and not something we put a lot of thought into. However, we are still responsible for our actions even if we don't put a lot of thought into them. Instead of just reacting, we can take control of our responses and find freedom from both external and internal forces that try to rob us of our ability to choose. The choice truly is ours, but sometimes our emotions get in the way.

To paraphrase a talk by Elder Lynn G. Robbins, Satan would like us to believe that we are victims of emotions we can't control. When we say something like, "You *make* me so mad," it sounds like we are not responsible for our actions. Someone else "made" us angry. This is a lie. We make the choice to be mad. No one can "make" us mad. Our kids may make a huge mess and our conditioned response is to yell at them. But our children didn't "make" us yell at them. The mess didn't "make" us yell about it. We chose to yell. Our power to choose is what sets us apart from other creatures on Earth. [15] Learning to act is better than being acted upon. [16]

So how do we learn to stay in control of our responses? We look to the Savior. He was able to stay calm when others around Him did all they could to catch Him off guard or "make" Him angry. The situations He faced were difficult and yet He stayed calm and compassionate and met the needs of others. How was He able to do this, and is there any way we can hope to do likewise?

Part of the answer lies in His daily habit of rising early and praying to His Father. His prayers not only aligned His will with His Father's, but they centered Him. Jesus was centered on the work His Father needed Him to do.

---

14   Stephen R. Covey, *Living the 7 Habits: Stories of Courage and Inspiration* (New York: Simon and Schuster, 1999), 21.

15   2 Nephi 2: 13-14.

16   Lynn G. Robbins, "Anger and Agency," *Ensign*, May 1998.

His prayers early in the morning may have helped to create space between difficult situations and the way He would respond later in His day. Jesus chose how He would respond. Jesus chose to act and not be acted upon.

When the scribes and Pharisees brought a woman who had been caught sinning to Jesus in the temple,[17] He stayed calm despite the harsh words the men threw around. Jesus didn't answer them right away. He wrote in the dirt and waited until they were quiet before He responded. Why did Jesus write in the dirt?

It may have been to give Him time to think of how He wanted to act instead of being acted upon. Jesus lengthened His response time by writing in the dirt, so when He did respond, He was cool and collected, and in complete control of His emotions.

We can lengthen our response time, too. When children are upset and the tension in the air makes us feel like our response needs to be immediate, we can slow it down by taking a deep breath, saying a quick prayer, and then moving forward with faith, trusting the Lord will help us respond in calm, positive ways. Our response changes if we let the Savior enter into this split-second or two. If we have prayed earlier in our day, picturing Him may be all we need to remind ourselves to respond in a Christlike way. We are more likely to let Him into this emotionally charged moment if we have a prayer in our hearts. His spirit helps us respond as He would.

When my kids were young, I wasn't sure which of my triggers to address first. I wanted to do better, but it was a bit overwhelming. Staying calm when my kids fought seemed like a good place to start. I made it a matter of prayer and contemplation. Instead of yelling to get their attention, I tried to listen to what they were fighting about, and then I waited until they noticed my presence. Because I was quiet, they would usually get quiet too, and then I could help them sort out the problem.

With my really young children who didn't understand a lot of words, I learned to pick up the smallest child so the physical fight stopped. I usually only said, "No fighting," as I walked to a quiet corner with them facing out until they quit crying. If the other child chose to hold on to my leg, I let them, but I didn't talk to them until they settled down. If they started hitting me, I tried to calmly take them to a designated place and told them to stay. (They knew the drill because we practiced this when everyone was calm. I pretended to be one of them and we role-played what would happen if they fought. I let them be me. They thought it was funny, but they also knew what my expectations were.) Intentionally thinking through my

---

17   John 8:1-12.

response to my children's fighting made it so we all knew what to expect. This technique tended to work for my young children when they fought.

After finding solutions to this problem, I prayerfully addressed other issues. (I'll give you a blueprint of how to do this in the workbook.) Please keep in mind, I still yelled when things caught me off guard, but I knew I was more in control than I had been. I felt joy knowing I had at least responded better some of the time, and I gradually decreased the amount of yelling I did and increased my ability to stay calm.

Here's another way I lengthened my response time when my teen didn't want to do a simple chore. I had a plan, and it made it easier for me to stay calm:

> Recently, I asked Janey to wash the dishes. She was not happy about the task and said, "I'm not washing the dishes!"
>
> I could have responded immediately with, "Oh, yes you are!" Instead, I took a breath, prayed for patience, and said, "I'm glad you know what your job is."
>
> She reminded me of how busy she was and that she didn't have time, and I said, "I know you're busy. Thanks for washing the dishes."
>
> She huffed, and I ignored it. I simply put some gloves by the sink and smiled a sympathetic smile as I walked out. I could hear her loudly getting ready to wash the dishes, but she was washing the dishes.
>
> Later that night, I thanked her for getting the job done and she said, "Sorry, I overreacted. It didn't take me that long." I smiled and hugged her. It felt good to lengthen the space before I responded by letting Jesus in with a quick prayer.

There are several examples of creating space before we respond throughout this book. The example given in Chapter Seven (the "joy" chapter) makes it easy to see the space created before a response is given. I suggest reading this experience if you need another example of creating space. It also gives you a glimpse of the blessings that come from following in the Savior's footsteps. This concept is going to take some time to sink in. Be patient and prayerful, and let the example of Jesus Christ help you lengthen the time between a trigger and your response. The workbook for this chapter will give you a chance to practice this game-changing concept.

Jesus took time to pray, reflect, and center Himself often. He didn't wait for a problem to arise before He decided to be calm. He had already made that decision during the time He spent with His Father. Jesus chose to act instead of reacting to His challenges. He was intentional in the way He lived

His life. His example can help us to change our way of dealing with difficult situations. When we make prayer a bigger part of our parenting solutions, things change, and we can feel peace and spread His light. Jesus loves us, knows our hearts, and wants us to counsel with our Heavenly Father. Jesus did this when He was on earth, and so can we. Heavenly Father wants to counsel with us about creating space to act. He wants to direct our paths for good and ease our burdens.

Time Out for a Bit of a Pep Talk

Here are a few things to keep in mind as you work on having a better response. This is going to take time! Be patient with yourself. Don't expect perfection. The challenges we face are tough, and we will not respond well every time! But we can learn to do things differently.

Acting instead of reacting to triggers is tough! This is not being brought up to frustrate you, or to give you an excuse to be extra hard on yourself. It is quite the opposite. Rely on the Savior and let Him guide you. Think about the person you would like to become. Instead of focusing on the things that didn't go well, recognize the things that were better. Being critical will only undermine your efforts. Learning new things takes time and requires effort. We will not get it right the first time, and that is OK. Be patient with yourself and be prayerful.

Many of my prayers have gone something like this, "Heavenly Father, you know I struggle with my responses to my children. And I struggled today! I need thy help to not lose my patience when the boys fight. I know I can do better. Wilt thou help me pause and think of thy Son before I respond . . . " Our Heavenly Father loves us and will help us with our responses.

This book is designed to help you see the Savior in a new way. He doesn't wait for us to make a mistake so He can make us feel bad. Satan is the one who wants us to be discouraged. Jesus looks for us to succeed and helps us feel good. In a later chapter, we will explore how Jesus is positive and always builds us up. The next chapter will help us understand how forgiveness is a necessary tool to have in our parenting toolbox. For now, let's dive into the workbook.

The Space Between

Workbook

There are ways to increase the space we have between a trigger (stimulus) and our response. The following workbook pages give us some ideas on how to increase this space. We know the Lord loves effort, so let's try our hand at being intentional about learning to act instead of reacting to the situations around us that try our patience and cause us grief. This is not for the faint at heart. It will require effort and honesty. But at the end of it, you will have the opportunity to know yourself and the Savior better as you learn to create a little wiggle room for yourself when it comes to your responses.

Spot Triggers

Just to get us started, let's look at what triggers us. Here is a list of common triggers for parents. Circle the top five triggers that cause your blood pressure to rise or you to have a reaction that is unkind or reflexive. Remember, when we pinpoint trouble spots, we can recognize them when they happen and practice creating a space so we can respond in calm, positive ways.

Siblings fighting	Whining	public
Raised voices	Crying	Nose picking
Children refusing to	Yelling	Child's eating habits
do what is asked	Whistling	Untamed hair
Messes	Yodeling	Child's performance
Out-of-place things	Technology issues	at school
like dirty socks,	Risky behaviors	Homework
dishes, etc.	Annoying behaviors	Can't find shoes
Noise levels	Child's behavior in	

What other triggers do you have that are not listed above?

_____

_____

_____

Did you finish your trigger list and realize you wanted to circle most or all of them (maybe not yodeling)? That is okay! There is this cool phenomenon that happens when we are willing to look at some of our triggers honestly. If you "fix" a few trouble spots, other trouble spots become less troublesome. It's called the snowball effect.

Picture a small snowball rolling down a snow-covered hill. It starts off small, but picks up more and more snow as it goes, making it larger and larger. The small efforts you are making in this workbook can cause the ball to move in the right direction. If you work through a couple of trouble spots, it may be enough to help other trouble spots disappear.

Choosing Better Responses to My Triggers

By looking at one of these trouble spots when you are calm and not worked up about it, you have a better chance of overcoming it. The list of your triggers may seem long, but do not lose courage! Choose one to use while working through the following steps. You can come back later and work through other triggers, but for now, just choose one.

1. What trigger would you like to work on? Why do you think it is a trigger for you?

_____

_____

_____

_____

2. How do you usually respond to this trigger? Be honest. This is for your eyes only.

_____

_____

_____

_____

3. How would you like to respond?

_____

_____

_____

_____

4. Did Jesus have a similar problem? How did He respond?

_____

_____

_____

5. See yourself responding similarly. Can you see yourself staying in control?

_____

_____

_____

Pray for help and create more space to act instead of reacting to your trigger. Give yourself credit and recognize efforts made by others and yourself to respond in a better way. When something happens that has triggered us before, we can create space between the stimulus and response by picturing the Savior and seeing ourselves handling the situation better.

We can pray for help in doing this. It's okay to talk to Heavenly Father about something we struggle with, even if it is about losing it over dirty dishes in the living room. He truly can help us with the small things *and* the big things that are plaguing us. Humbly coming to Him with our burdens gives Him a chance to lighten them.

When one of your triggers happens, try the following:

    a.   Take a moment to breathe. . . you've got this!
    b.   Pray for strength, and picture the Savior.
    c.   Remember, you are in control.

d. You can be calm even when others choose otherwise.

e. Let yourself pause to act in calm, loving ways instead of answering with anger or annoyance. Jesus wrote in the dirt and waited until the Pharisees and scribes quit yelling. Put away groceries or find something in your purse while you wait for children to calm down. It only takes being calm three times when someone tries to engage us in an argument to dispel the other person's anger.

f. Remember to let compassion and love rule your actions.

Chapter Four

Forgiving and Forgetting

In a moment of frustration, parents may say something like, "I've told you a thousand times to not leave your shoes in the middle of the floor!" This all-too-familiar offense highlights a problem many of us have with forgiveness. Why do we feel the need to remind our children of their shortcomings and thoughtlessness? Aren't we supposed to forgive and forget?

These seemingly small offenses give us a chance to show we understand a foundational principle of forgiveness. When others have made a mistake, we are to remember them no more. If we are to forgive seventy times seven, we might start with not making such a big deal about finding shoes in the middle of the floor.

If we stop to look at our child's faces when we express our frustration over misplaced shoes, we may see their countenance crumble. Our kids may be surprised by our anger. They may have been happily playing with their matchbox cars in the corner when we started yelling. In the child's mind, he may be thinking, "I didn't do it on purpose. I'll never do it right! I was just in a hurry to play with my new matchbox car." Especially when other similar comments will probably come his way in the future. What message are we sending our children about forgiveness if we hold grudges in this way? Why do we make ourselves so mad about misplaced shoes?

Something seems to trigger in our brain, and we react (see Chapter 3). These angry responses are said with such malice that kids feel they will never get it right. Kids have probably been leaving shoes where they shouldn't from the time we started wearing shoes, but that does not mean our level of annoyance should reflect this. Other children's mistakes should not be heaped on our sons' or daughters' shoulders. They have not misplaced their shoes a thousand times. So why does our tone sound so annoyed and frustrated? Are we heaping all of their siblings' mistakes on them as well? Or our frustrations from a long day? Did we just need to yell about something?

Let's take a second look at the words we are throwing at our kids. First, it's not a crime to leave shoes lying around. It's a mistake and one a lot of us make. (Admit it. We do it too.) The shoe problem can be addressed, but let's put the mistake into perspective. We do our children a disservice when we don't forgive them for past mistakes or the mistakes of others.

Sometimes we feel obligated to be annoyed by things our children do so they know it's something they shouldn't do. But is this forgiving? Jesus said we should forgive others seventy times seven. That's a lot. If we are to forgive and remember their sins no more, should our tone of voice sound so annoyed? There are better ways to deal with kids being oblivious to the mess they create or the fact that their sandwich is dripping jelly all over the floor. We don't have to get upset just to let our kids know they made a mistake.

Jesus has given us many examples and parables about how to forgive others. His examples can help us forgive the big hurts and the small hurts that come our way during this life. We can learn a great deal about forgiveness and extending mercy from Jesus. He shows us that when mistakes are made, we can help people to progress by giving them a chance to repent and move on. He offers us forgiveness and gives the promise that if we repent, turn back to Him, and sin no more, He will remember our sins no more.

We can do this for family members by politely asking our kids to put their shoes in the basket, or even noticing the shoes already in the basket. This lets them know good gets your attention too. When children make mistakes like leaving their shoes in the middle of the floor, we can be forgiving and offer mercy by remembering it no more. Cease to bring it up again and move on. Don't hold it over their head for the next three years. Forgiveness simply remembers the offense no more.

Practice Forgiving

Instead of practicing holding a grudge, we can practice forgiving. We don't want our kids to be good at holding grudges. We want them to be good at forgiving others. Our home can be a place where forgiveness is freely offered and mercy is extended to all. We can make our home a safe place to practice these needed skills in civility. We can't expect children to automatically know how to forgive if they haven't tried it out and learned how wonderful it feels to forgive and forget the wrongdoings of others or be on the receiving end of forgiveness. Learning improves when children see a principle in action. Our example teaches them about forgiveness. What are they learning?

We can teach them that through the Atonement of Jesus Christ, sins can be forgiven. Mistakes can be forgotten. Forgiveness of sins can bring about relief from burdens and even joy. Or we can teach them that making mistakes causes others to be resentful, harsh, and downright mean, or maybe it just depends on the day or what mood we are in. Childhood is designed for making mistakes. Parents can use this as a time to let kids practice and learn from their mistakes.

Elder Lynn G. Robbins reminds us that mistakes are part of the learning process. He says, "Mistakes are a fact of life. Learning to skillfully play the piano is essentially impossible without making thousands of mistakes—maybe even a million. To learn a foreign language, one must face the embarrassment of making thousands of mistakes—maybe even a million. Even the world's greatest athletes never stop making mistakes."[18] Putting shoes away could be added to the list of things that need practice to perfect.

Our kids need us to move on and not hold a grudge. This can be hard since we often deal with the same problems day in and day out. We don't have to let them know having shoes in the middle of the floor is one of our triggers. We can resist the urge to get angry and just stay calm. We can keep our tone of voice pleasant when we ask them to pick up their shoes. They may never know the inner turmoil we face when we choose not to "lose it" about shoes, but we know we resisted the urge to get upset and this feels so good!

Our home can be a place to practice forgiving others. When my two oldest were small, we were talking about forgiveness in Family Home Evening, and out of the blue, Sydney hit her brother. We were shocked at first. This was unprovoked and such a random thing to do. Next thing we knew, Sydney started instructing Thory on what he was supposed to say. "Now Thory, I'm going to say I am sorry for hitting you. You need to say, 'I forgive you.' Then I will work to be sorry and not do it again." She said it so matter-of-factly it was hard not to laugh. Kerry and I let them "practice" a few more times (minus the hard slug in the arm) until Sydney let us know she understood the concept. Kids need chances to practice forgiving in a safe environment.

They need to see forgiveness in action. These seemingly insignificant things allow us opportunities to teach. We can model how to be forgiving, positive, and understanding about where our children are developmentally.

---

18   Lynn G. Robbins, "Until Seventy Times Seven," *Ensign*, May 2018.

We can pray for strength to forgive those who have wronged us, and abandon feelings of anger, bitterness, and revenge. We can look for the good in others, rather than focusing on their faults and magnifying their weaknesses. Remember, the rule of Thumper's mom from *Bambi*, "If you can't say somethin' nice, don't say nothin' at all." God will be the judge of others' harmful or often thoughtless actions. We are to forgive.

Admitting When We're Wrong

Sometimes we struggle to admit when we are wrong. We may think our kids should never see us making mistakes because then they won't respect our authority. The opposite is actually true. Respect comes from being respectful. If we want our children to respect us we should treat them with respect by respectfully talking to them. This encourages children to also talk to us respectfully. Children respect parents more if they can admit when they are wrong.

Our children need to see us making mistakes (lots of them) and working through the aftermath. No matter their age, they need to see us asking for forgiveness and working hard to not repeat the offense, and when we are too harsh, they need to see us being humble and asking for forgiveness and turning back to God. Admitting our mistakes shows children that mistakes happen. What we do to make them right gives us a chance to practice being Christlike.

One of my earliest memories of my grandma was seeing her get down on the ground where I was playing with some wooden bowls and apologize to me. Her apology was simple, "I'm sorry I yelled at you. I was worried you were up too high in the tree. I thought you were going to get hurt. Will you forgive me?" I remember I wrapped my arms around her, and said simply, "Grandma, I was up too high."

Children are quick to forgive and naturally show mercy when given a chance. One thing childhood is for is to learn the process of forgiving and forgetting. We would be wise to not shy away from the simple things that happen every day that give us opportunities to teach principles that can stay with an individual for a lifetime.

President Henry B. Eyring said it this way, "Because none of us is perfect and feelings are easily hurt, families can become sacred sanctuaries only as we repent early and sincerely. Parents can set an example. Harsh words or unkind thoughts can be repented of quickly and sincerely. A simple 'I am sorry' can heal wounds and invite both forgiveness and love."[19]

---

19   Henry B. Eyring, "A Home Where the Spirit of the Lord Dwells," *Ensign*, May 2019.

Children benefit from receiving mercy and forgiveness from their parents. This helps them to learn what it sounds like, looks like, and feels like to not hold a grudge. This helps them learn what it takes to be forgiving. Creating an atmosphere in our home where forgiveness and mercy are freely shared feels good. We want both to be a natural part of our home. Joy comes from creating a place where these things can be learned and practiced.

Thinking about the everyday chances we have to show forgiveness and mercy prepares us to deal with harder things. There are weightier issues we deal with because we are a part of a family. This can be difficult because the hurt is often great. The same principles can be applied to the weightier matters we encounter. Let's dive a little deeper into what it means to forgive. Let's spend some time at the Master's feet to understand how forgiveness and mercy can play a bigger role in our family life.

Showing Forgiveness and Mercy

Jesus came to earth to make forgiveness possible. Mistakes can be righted. Hearts can be mended and burdens can be lifted. Jesus showed us how to do this. He forgave people of their trespasses and showed us a better way.

The story of the prodigal son helps us to understand more about forgiveness.[20] This story appears to be about a son returning to his family after making a series of poor decisions that caused him to lose his inheritance, but if we look deeper, we can see that it is about all of us. We are the prodigal, hoping to return home to our Heavenly Father.

The father in this parable meets his wayward son when he is still a great way off. This is a tender scene and one that we hope will be repeated when we return home. Our Father will meet us when we are a great way off with open arms because He wants us to return to Him. Our choices can separate us from Him, but when we turn back, He will welcome us. He is safe and familiar to us. Turning back also implies that our hearts are humble and we are willing to submit our will to His. In the parable, we see the son physically returning home, but we get a glimpse that his circumstances humbled him and caused him to have a change of heart.

We gain further insight into why our Heavenly Father is so willing to welcome us home by what the father in this story says to his other son, who is having a hard time opening his arms to his brother. The answer the father gives this faithful, but slow-to-forgive brother is memorable: ". . . Son, thou art ever with me, and all that I have is thine. It was meet that we should

---

20   Luke 15: 11-32.

make merry, and be glad: for this thy brother was dead, and is alive again; and was lost, and is found."[21]

The father welcomes the son home because he was lost and is now found. The son has been humbled, so mercy can be extended to him. We hope that he continues to make progress, but for now, we'll welcome him home and acknowledge he made a step in the right direction, even if continuing in that way remains to be seen. Jesus talks of the father coming out when his son is still a long way off, suggesting that the father forgave quickly, if not instantly. He sends the message to the son that he loves him and is glad to see him again. This is a good reminder for us to forgive quickly as well as extend mercy to the wrongdoer. (I am not suggesting putting yourself in an unsafe place with an abuser, but simply thinking about extending mercy.)

This is a touchy subject for far too many of us. It is hard to lose someone we care deeply about to the world and its enticements. This is an agonizing road to go down. Many want to forgive and open their arms to a prodigal, but does that mean we have to let them live with us again?

No, but we can turn the hurt over to God. Forgiveness frees our hearts and gives us a chance to rely on the infinite Atonement of Jesus Christ. Jesus is the one that makes forgiveness possible. He is the bridge that helps us return to our Father in Heaven. Jesus will meet us where we are and provide a way for the prodigal to return.

Dealing with wayward family members is such an agonizing thing. Love, guilt, denial, anger, and many other emotions get tangled into us forgiving loved ones who may or may not have repented of past wrongs. Each of us in this type of situation will have to navigate what the prodigal's return, if any, may look like. Safety factors become particularly critical in situations involving potential drug abuse or other forms of abuse. Prodigals may also have a different definition of what being forgiving looks like. Desperate people can often talk a good talk, but walking their talk is a different ball game. Wrapping our arms around a prodigal is different than trusting them without defining boundaries for the wanderer. Having our hearts free may help us to help them move on to repenting of their wrongs, but that may take time and effort by all involved.

I know many are struggling with wayward children and we ache over choices they have made. We can look to the Savior in even these instances. He will ease our burdens if we let Him. I know we would like to "fix" our loved ones or at least help them to see the error of their ways, but they have their agency and have to make their own decisions about when, how, and if

---

21   Luke 15: 31-32.

they return to the Father. Jesus has the job of saving the lost sheep. We are sometimes asked to be His hands, but sometimes we have to turn it over to Him. "There is comfort in knowing His job is to save, our job is to love."[22]

What If It Is Hard to Forgive?

Forgiving others is difficult. However, like most things, the more we practice, the easier it will be. James E. Faust found this definition of forgiveness that gives us a bigger picture of what it is, he said, "Dr. Sidney Simon has provided an excellent definition of forgiveness as it applies to human relationships: 'Forgiveness is freeing up and putting to better use the energy once consumed by holding grudges, harboring resentments, and nursing unhealed wounds. It is rediscovering the strengths we always had and relocating our limitless capacity to understand and accept other people and ourselves.'"

President Faust goes on to say, "Most of us need time to work through pain and loss. We can find all manner of reasons for postponing forgiveness. One of these reasons is waiting for the wrongdoers to repent before we forgive them. Yet such a delay causes us to forfeit the peace and happiness that could be ours. The folly of rehashing long-past hurts does not bring happiness. Some hold grudges for a lifetime, unaware that courageously forgiving those who have wronged us is wholesome and therapeutic."[23]

Forgiving others takes courage and is good for the soul. We don't have to wait until the wrongdoer has repented. Keeping our hearts soft is more important than having the other person admit we were right, or that they hurt us. Rehashing past hurts will not bring us happiness. Forgiveness frees our hearts from these heavy burdens. My friend, Ellie, gives us a glimpse of what forgiveness can look like in the following example.

> *Ellie has had a rocky relationship with her mother for years. It surprised me when she told me she was going to California to be with her mother. When I asked her what had changed she said, "Hopefully, me. I realized that most of the things that made it hard for me to be with my mother were still going to be there and I couldn't change them, but I can change my reaction to them. I'm working on not letting them affect me as they have in the past. I'm concentrating on the good things."*
>
> *Then I said, "It sounds like you've been able to forgive her for the hurts she has caused you."*

---

22   Andrea Palmer, "Lesson 9 - Thought Habit #7 - I Have Power Over What I Think-Feel-Do," *Worth of Souls Podcast.*

23   James E. Faust, "The Healing Power of Forgiveness," *Ensign*, May 2007.

Her answer was simple, "Yes, and this will be the test to see if I can rely on the Lord to help me not feel the old hurts."

When she came home, we talked about her experience. She said, "My mom is still my mom, but with the Lord's help, it didn't bother me. The Lord helped me to see that her comments were her way of showing concern and love for me. I wish she would change, but I'm not letting it bother me anymore."

Ellie's willingness to forgive gave her a new perspective on an old hurt, and that perspective has made all the difference.

It's hard to forgive someone who has not changed, but Ellie's story helps us see it is possible. The Lord can soften our hearts if we invite Him in. He may even help us see things with fresh eyes. Jesus loves us and does not want us to carry heavy burdens. We don't need to impress Him with our strength. He wants to ease our burdens by taking on our hurts and pains. Let Him do His job! Unburden yourself and let Him carry and change your heavy heart.

If it is really hard, we can remember the example Jesus set for us in the last moments of His life. One of the Savior's last acts was to forgive the soldiers that hung Him on the cross. These hardened soldiers had a horrible job and they were cruel. They did not understand that they were killing the one who could save them all. But the Savior knew they did not comprehend the magnitude of what they were doing, and amid His terrible pain, He pled with the Father saying, ". . . forgive them; for they know not what they do."[24] In our agony, can we forgive others who have unknowingly or knowingly hurt us? Jesus forgave. He didn't want anything weighing on His heart. Can we be like Jesus in this? If He can forgive His trespassers, then so can we.

There are so many things people do on accident, or out of ignorance that cause pain and hurt. Maybe loved ones are a bit too opinionated about how we choose to live our lives, or maybe we have been wrongly accused of something. These things can be hard to bear.

Some of us may wonder if forgiveness is possible after abuse. Help from this burden can be found in the healing power of the Savior's Atonement. The Lord loves us and wants to help us through these hard things. If you are struggling and need help, reach out to a professional or someone you trust. You can be free from these heavy burdens with time and patience.

Christ's example of forgiving others can help us be more forgiving. To be more like the Savior, we could say something like, "I can forgive them, for they know not what they do." May we be quick(er) to forgive. Jesus loves

---

24   JST Luke 23:35.

us and can carry our burdens. He will not forget us, for we are written upon His hands.[25]

Letting Go of Parenting Mistakes

Do you have a hard time forgiving yourself? Do you dwell on your perceived shortcomings? We all have them. We make mistakes as we learn, especially when we are learning something new like parenting. If we beat ourselves up for past mistakes, it can make something like parenting harder. Learning to forgive ourselves can be tricky.

Parenting is a tough job because many of us carry extra burdens from past parenting mistakes, unrealistic expectations we've set for ourselves, or unexpected things out of our control. Some carry burdens leftover from childhood that we are trying to change for our own children, but change is hard. The Savior really is the answer to these concerns.

Forgiveness can play a more vital role in our families and make our time together more enjoyable. Forgiveness and mercy work hand in hand to help us have new days and new chances. Parenting mistakes are part of the territory. The best thing we can do for ourselves and our children is to learn from our mistakes and figure out ways to avoid making the mistake again. If you are feeling bad about something you did, you might as well work to put it behind you and not beat yourself up about it.

Like all mistakes, the forgiveness process is the same for parenting mistakes. The secret is to not get stuck just feeling bad. Many of us get stuck feeling bad about our parenting mistakes. We think we have done something about it because we have felt bad. Then, when it happens again, we may feel even worse, and the cycle continues. Instead, we can ask for forgiveness, if necessary, and let those feelings of remorse spur us to make some changes. Satan would have us believe change is impossible, but Jesus can show us the way.

Forgive yourself and move on to face the current challenges you have with courage. Today can be a new day for us, with God's help! Remember, we can put past mistakes in the past and leave them there. If there is something really grievous, repent of it, turn back to God, and move on. Look to the Savior for help. He is the perfect example of how to live. When you feel you are going to fall short, rely on Him. Jesus will help you get to a better place. Have patience with yourself and let Him be your guide.

We can forgive ourselves and move on. We don't have to get stuck just feeling bad. We don't have to carry these burdens alone. Jesus wants to do His job of relieving our burdens and we can let Him. He knows we are strong and

---

25   1 Nephi 21:16.

willing to do hard things, but carrying this weight is not one of them. We need to get the notion out of our heads that Jesus and others will be impressed with the burdens we are carrying. He will not. Let Him do His job.

It's hard to get past our parenting mistakes. Maybe the problem seems too large to tackle and we have no energy left, or we can't see a way to change our current situation. Any of these reasons make it so we deal with the same struggles at the same time day after day. Blaming our children for our frustrations happens a lot. It is easier to blame someone else. We all do that, but we can learn a better way.

There are several places throughout this book that give you a chance to work through parenting issues. I hope you will do this. It feels amazing to unravel a trouble spot in our day and do what we can to change it so we don't make the same mistakes repeatedly. For now, use the space in the workbook to be intentional about forgiving yourself and moving on. Our backpack is already heavy enough. Remove some rocks in yours and see how good it makes you feel.

Intentional Forgiveness
Workbook

This chapter gave us a glimpse into how Jesus forgives. Ponder on these and other instances Jesus showed us how to forgive. Write about your findings in the space below.

1. What do you understand better about forgiveness because of the Savior's example?

_____

_____

_____

_____

2. How did the Savior forgive others?

_____

_____

_____

_____

3. How can you forgive as the Savior does?

_____

_____

_____

_____

4. What does forgiveness look like daily in your family?

_____

_____

_____

_____

5. Do you hold grudges? If so, how can you practice forgiveness instead?

_____

_____

_____

_____

_____

_____

6. What large and small things are weighing on your heart? How can you free your heart from these burdens?

_____

_____

_____

_____

Hidden Wedges

A few years ago, President Monson gave a talk entitled "Hidden Wedges."[26] In this talk he explained that "hidden wedges" are hidden hurts or grudges we hold in our hearts. If these hard feelings are never put to rest, they can cause us to carry resentment instead of love for a person, a family, a church, or even ourselves. In this section, we will work on putting to rest the hidden wedges in our hearts. Learning to forgive others is hard to do, but when we are intentional we can free our hearts of these burdens.

President Monson loved to tell a good story to help us understand more about the Savior's gospel. He told a story about an ice storm that caused the branches of a walnut tree to split and then fall to the ground. This stumped the white-haired farmer. He knew walnut trees could usually withstand a storm like the one they had experienced. When he investigated, he found a feller's wedge that had been left between branches when the tree was younger. The tree had grown around it. This wedge weakened the tree and caused it to break.

President Monson then takes the story deeper, when he says the following, "There are hidden wedges in the lives of many whom we know— yes, perhaps in our own families." He felt that "hidden wedges" could be removed with effort, forgiveness, and mercy.

Let's look at where they originate. President Monson says, "Some come from unresolved disputes, which lead to ill feelings, followed by remorse and regret. Others find their beginnings in disappointments, jealousies, arguments, and imagined hurts. We must solve them—lay them to rest and not leave them to canker, fester, and ultimately destroy."[27]

Work through the questions below and take time to remove a wedge from your heart. Think of the hidden hurts or unresolved disputes with

---

26   Thomas S. Monson, "Hidden Wedges," _Ensign_, May 2002.

27   Ibid.

family members you would like to put to rest. Free your heart from this type of burden.

1. What "hidden wedges" would you like to put to rest?

_____

_____

_____

_____

2. Are there "hidden wedges" in your heart for one of your children, a parent, or a sibling?

_____

_____

_____

_____

3. Is it hard to be around this person because they said or did something unkind or wrong? What happened?

_____

_____

_____

_____

4. Is this "hidden wedge" causing a rift between you and the other person?

_____

_____

_____

_____

5. Can you go to this person and make amends? (If the offense is serious, like abuse of any nature, work with someone you trust to make this decision. Know that you are loved! May you feel that love as you work to put hard things behind you.)

_____

_____

_____

_____

6. Is the person aware of the offense they committed? Do they need to be made aware of your hurt feelings for you to get over this hurt? Is this hurt going to be helped if you tell them you were hurt? Why?

_____

_____

_____

_____

Keep in mind, many offenses are none of the other person's business. This might sound strange. Here's an example. If you are sensitive about your ears, and a casual acquaintance makes a joke about ears and offends you because, as a child, people made fun of your ears, should you be mad at that acquaintance for making the joke? What if they didn't know about your sensitivity?

Ask yourself honestly if your grudge is over something they are clueless about. Being sensitive about your ears was something you struggled with as a child. It is none of their business unless you make it their business. You can put this behind you as an adult.

A way of looking at the joke is to let it remind you of how far you have come. We don't have to like the joke, but we can see that it wasn't intended to hurt us. It may help us to think about one of those hurtful moments from the past and let the strong, loving adult you are now comfort the hurt inner child. You are an adult now and can handle a friend talking about ears. If it still hurts, pray for help and let the true comforter comfort you.

Think about the hurt and ask yourself if it is worth letting this hurt affect your life, health, or happiness. If it is not worth holding onto, now is the time to get down on your knees, unburden your heart, and extend mercy to this person for bringing up old hurts.

You really don't have to bring the other person into this conversation. Most likely they didn't mean to bring up a sensitive subject to offend you. They just thought they were being funny. If you feel hurt, pray to relieve your heart of this hurt. It feels so good to unburden your heart!

1. Do I need to distance myself from this person to work through some of my feelings for a while or can I work through this with the Lord's help now? Remember, we don't want to carry this burden any longer than we have to.

_____

_____

_____

_____

2. Am I ready to ask the Lord to help me forgive this person?

_____

_____

_____

_____

3. Is there new information about the situation I need to figure in? Do I need to change my thinking about the person's intent?

_____

_____

_____

_____

4. Am I reading things into the person's motives? Should I pray to change my mindset? Am I looking for the person to offend me so I can continue to be mad? Do I need something to be mad about and they are my target?

_____

_____

_____

_____

5. What would be best for me to do, even if it is hard?

_____

_____

_____

_____

I'd like to share an experience that helped me learn to forgive daily and not hold grudges. I took similar steps to forgive someone that I felt had wronged me. It has served as an example and helped my husband and I to avoid needless "hidden wedges."

When Kerry and I were first married, we were students at Utah State University and we worked with a friend of ours named Jessie. We often had dinner with Jessie. He always complimented me on the meal and would tell me what a wonderful homemaker I was becoming.

I should have enjoyed his compliments, but I didn't. Looking back, I can see that I was sensitive about my new role as wife and future mother, and I wasn't sure how getting my education was going to fit into the new direction my life had taken when we got married. Unbeknownst to Jessie, he had become the target of my concerns and worries about my new role.

One day after Jessie had been especially complimentary, I was at my limit and said to Kerry. "Can you believe him? He doesn't think I will be good at anything else but cooking and cleaning. I have a brain!!!"

I remember Kerry looking at me in confusion. He said something like, "He was just letting you know the food was good." I went to reply but realised Kerry was right. I needed to quit assuming every compliment Jessie gave me about my cooking was a slight instead of a compliment. Our conversation gave me new information about Jessie's compliments, and I had a choice. I could see things the way they really were, or I could hold on to my grudge.

The next time Jessie complimented me, it wasn't easy to accept because the old feelings were still there. I hadn't forgiven him. I worked hard to absorb the new insight I had and prayed I could forgive Jessie and myself. With God's help, I knew I could forgive him and not put everything he said into a box labeled: "Chauvinistic." I was able to forgive Jessie and myself, and learned so much from the experience.

Kerry and I refer back to this often to help us avoid making the same mistake again. I have been able to laugh at my assumptions and am grateful the Lord enabled us to recognize a valuable aspect of the forgiveness process. Namely, just because I am sensitive about something doesn't make everything people say to me a cut or a slight.

The other thing I learned is that many times the hurts we suffer are things others may never know. Jessie intended to compliment me on my cooking. What I heard was that he thought I was only going to be good at homemaking. The people around us are not responsible for how we interpret things. We are responsible, and we shouldn't assume the worst about others and harbor hurt feelings.

Harboring hurt feelings in families takes on many forms. Some people lash out, while others keep their hurt feelings inside and quietly stew. Watch for signs of this with your children. These big feelings may be hard for them to navigate. Giving children at any age a sounding board helps them work through their feelings. Kerry did this for me without even realizing it. Hearing how "off" my thoughts were helped me to realize I was misjudging Jessie. Interpretations about others around us can be off, and having a listening ear helps loved ones to not create "hidden wedges."

Forgiving Yourself

The story above revealed a "hidden wedge" I had in my heart. My thinking was off and working through my grudge gave me a chance to forgive someone for saying things I thought were offensive. He hopefully never knew his compliments frustrated me. My frustrations were mine to deal with.

We can also have "hidden wedges" in our hearts against ourselves. We hold grudges towards ourselves that we repeat in our minds, and this can erode our confidence, our faith, and our relationships with others—especially our family members. Mistakes come with being on this earth.

Sherene Van Dyke | 55

Working through them is freeing. We can work through hidden hurts to free our hearts so there is more room for love. These hard feelings that we never put to rest about ourselves can cause us to carry resentment instead of love for ourselves. We can stop telling ourselves these hurtful things and forgive ourselves.

We are our own worst critic. We can be extra hard on ourselves and tend to get stuck feeling bad about our real or perceived shortcomings. Getting stuck saying negative things to ourselves only makes us more discouraged. Instead of putting ourselves down when we have made a mistake, we can look at it as an opportunity to grow.

When I was trying to change my responses to my children to be more positive, I was critical of every mistake I made. Then I realized that my kids were not the only ones that needed me to be more positive. At the end of the day instead of reminding myself of all the times I had messed up, I tried to remember the times my responses were more in control and positive. Training my eyes to see these times helped me to make the changes I wanted to make. We can be more forgiving of ourselves.

The questions below are to help you work through any "hidden wedges" you have in your heart towards yourself. The Lord loves you and He can help you ease the burdens that are weighing on your hearts. You can take or leave what is offered below, but work to forgive yourself.

1. What "hidden wedges" would you like to put to rest about yourself? What do you have a hard time forgiving yourself for?

_____

_____

_____

_____

2. Is there something you did in the past that causes you to feel pain?

_____

_____

_____

_____

3. Is this "hidden wedge" affecting your relationship with one of your family members?

_____

_____

_____

_____

4. Is this " hidden wedge" affecting your confidence as a parent, sibling, or friend? Are you ready to forgive yourself?

_____

_____

_____

_____

5. Is this "hidden wedge" causing a rift between you and another person?

_____

_____

_____

_____

6. Can you forgive yourself and move on? (If the offense is serious, like abuse of any nature, work with someone you trust. Know that you are loved! May you feel the love that Heavenly Father and Jesus Christ have for you as you work to put hard things behind you.)

_____

_____

_____

_____

7. Is there new information about the situation you need to figure in? Do you need to change your thinking about what happened in the past?

_____

_____

_____

_____

8. Are you looking to keep this hurt alive in your heart as punishment for the mistake you made or think you made?

_____

_____

_____

_____

_____

_____

_____

9. Can you ask Heavenly Father to help you forgive yourself?

_____

_____

_____

_____

_____

_____

_____

Chapter Five

Jesus Is Positive

"Our Savior, Jesus Christ, always builds us up and never tears us down."[28] This statement can cause us to think, "Is Jesus always positive? Does He always build us up?" We can scour the scriptures and see that this statement is true (I have done this and know it is true). The interactions He has with others throughout the scriptures show us this, and this knowledge can bring our hearts great joy. Jesus brings so much light into our lives. He truly builds us up and never tears us down. Our families need us to do likewise.

The Savior found positive ways to encourage people throughout the scriptures. He reminds them of their potential and acknowledges their effort in following Him and our Heavenly Father. We find some of His most positive responses in Third Nephi.[29] Jesus expresses His joy with the Nephites and lets them know He is well pleased with them. His words at that time were about specific things they had done. It didn't take many words to express His positive feelings. It would have been wonderful to be there and witness His joy. His love and joy came through the words He said. His words benefited those present and those reading the account in the scriptures. Our words can benefit our children similarly. If we want to have a positive impact on our loved ones, we can learn to look for the good in them.

President Gordon B. Hinckley was a very wise and positive leader of the Church of Jesus Christ of Latter-day Saints. His advice to let optimism replace pessimism could help us be more positive with our family members.

---

28   Dallin H. Oaks, "The Atonement and Faith," *Ensign*, May 2010.
29   See 3 Nephi 18:10; 27:30

I am asking that we stop seeking out the storms and enjoy more fully the sunlight. I am suggesting that as we go through life we 'accentuate the positive.' I am asking that we look a little deeper for the good, that we still voices of insult and sarcasm, that we more generously compliment virtue and effort. . . What I am suggesting is that each of us turn from the negativism that so permeates our society and look for the remarkable good among those with whom we associate, that we speak of one another's virtues more than we speak of one another's faults, that optimism replace pessimism, that our faith exceed our fears.[30]

His words remind us we should be different from the rest of the world. Negativism is everywhere, but it does not need to be a part of our homes. Instead, we can speak of the virtues of those we love.

According to parent educator Dr. Glenn L. Latham, "Parents typically ignore 95-97 percent of all the appropriate and good things their children do. But if a child misbehaves, parents are five to six times more likely to pay attention to that behavior. When parents only respond to the negative things children do, no one should be surprised that the children misbehave because children tend to repeat behaviors that draw their parents' attention."[31]

Why do we ignore the good and pay attention to our children when they misbehave? With practice, we can train our eyes to see the good. We strengthen the behaviors we give our attention to. If we want to see whining, crying, lying, etc., continue to give children our attention for doing these things. If we want to see our children being kind, trustworthy, and honest, we need to "catch 'em being good."

It is much better to catch our children being good than to catch them being bad. Dr. Latham also said, "The most effective way to teach children to behave well is to strengthen desirable behavior through positive reinforcement. The least effective way to reduce problem behavior is through the use of averse or negative processes (yelling, spanking, etc.)"[32]

Then why do we fail to see the good in our children and concentrate on their mistakes? We seem to have the mistaken belief that we have to "fix" our children. That is just not the case. We think that by pointing out their flaws, kids will fix the flaws we point out, but the opposite is often true. We actually strengthen the behaviors we acknowledge. Maybe we are afraid

30   Gordon B. Hinckley, "The Continuing Pursuit of Truth," *Ensign*, May 1986.
31   Dr. Glenn L. Latham, *What's a Parent to Do*, (Salt Lake City: Deseretbook, 1997), 116.
32   Dr. Glenn L. Latham, *The Power of Positive Parenting*, (Logan: P&T Ink, 1993), 19.

that if we don't point out flaws, we're not being good parents. Simply notice when they are behaving appropriately. Thank them for picking up their shoes instead of yelling at them for having shoes in the middle of the floor.

It really is about timing and learning to "catch 'em doin' good" things. Our children need to know that we are looking for them to succeed and not to fail. We send this message to them by focusing on things that build them up. It's not that hard to say, "I noticed that you picked up your shoes, thank you! Or I noticed you were kind to your little brother." Noticing the good in our children is so simple! Learning to ignore the inappropriate behaviors of our children is wise, but difficult. It's easier to notice the shoes in the middle of the floor than to wait until the child picks them up.

Children want us to pay attention to them. Our attention is one of the most powerful motivators we have. Children will do what it takes to get noticed, leading many to misbehave. Here's an example from Primary.

Aaron, a three-year-old boy, chose to lie down on the floor where the primary chorister needed to walk to lead the music during Primary. He had been doing this for a couple of Sundays. The music leader and various other leaders had tried to convince him he needed to sit in his chair. They had given him a lot of attention for his unacceptable behavior. No matter what they said to him, his behavior did not change. He was still lying on the floor.

The music leader was unsure of what to do but decided to try something different. She asked all the other adults to ignore him and she would take care of the problem. The chorister placed all her attention on the children that were behaving well. She thanked the children for sitting on their chairs, smiled at them, and thanked others for smiling at her, but ignored Aaron. She even stepped over him once and acted as if it was no big deal that he was lying on the floor.

About seven minutes into Singing Time, Aaron stood up, put his hands on his hips, and huffed as he said, "Aren't you going to notice me?!"

The music leader calmly said, "I will when you are sitting on your chair." He huffed and puffed all the way to his chair, but then he sat there. The music leader calmly knelt in front of him and thanked him for sitting on his chair. He never laid on the floor again because the music leader made sure she noticed his good behavior and had positive interactions with him and the other members of the Primary. By ignoring this age-typical behavior, the music leader helped the behavior to go away.

Here's another example:

One father decided he was tired of his seven-year-old daughter's whining. Every evening between six and seven, he decided he would not pay attention to his daughter when she whined. (He just didn't speak "whine.") He explained what would get his attention and did not engage with her when she whined. When she wasn't whining, he would smile and talk with her. When the father turned his attention to her strengths instead of her weaknesses, the whining went away, and not just between six and seven. If she happened to whine, he gently reminded her to use her nice voice, and he would be glad to listen.

Both examples illustrate the power of paying attention to the positive and ignoring the negative. We can reinforce desirable behavior by simply showing interest in what our children are doing. There are many ways we can interact with our loved ones in positive ways, like smiling, expressing gratitude, or giving them a pat on the back. Praise should be genuine and directed at the child's behavior and its value to you and others. For example, "I appreciate your help cleaning the kitchen" or "I enjoy our time together." Praise directed at children like, "You're such a good boy" may come across as insincere or manipulative.

President Russell M. Nelson gave us a recent example of how to be positive while teaching us the expectations for appropriate behavior during the announcement of new temples. In the workbook for this section, there is a step-by-step plan for better behavior ("Five Steps to Better Behavior"). Compare the instruction President Nelson gives to this plan. See if you can pick out the steps involved in influencing behavior positively.

As we have discussed here tonight, you sisters are vital to the work of the temple, and the temple is where you will receive your highest spiritual treasures.

Please listen carefully and reverently as I will now announce plans to build eight new temples. If one is announced in a place that is meaningful to you, I suggest that you simply bow your head prayerfully with gratitude in your heart. We are pleased to announce plans to construct temples in the following locations: Freetown, Sierra Leone; Orem, Utah; Port Moresby, Papua New Guinea; Bentonville, Arkansas; Bacolod, Philippines; McAllen, Texas; Cobán, Guatemala; and Taylorsville, Utah. Thank you, dear sisters. We deeply appreciate your receipt of these plans and your reverent response.[33]

33   Russell M. Nelson, "Spiritual Treasures," *Ensign*, October 2019.

President Nelson found a positive way to help us know the proper way to respond to temple construction announcements. Did you take the time to dissect how he did this? It was simple, positive, and effective. His approach is a great example of how to help others have better behavior. In our excitement about new temples, it became a bit of a contest to see who could outdo the level of enthusiasm for the new temples. He addressed this issue the next time he announced some new temples. He stopped, redirected, and then reinforced the appropriate response. It was pleasant, brief, and descriptive.

We can think of the behaviors we would like to see changed and use the five steps to better behavior to help us teach our children in a more Christlike way. A chart has been made to walk you through the process. Plug in your situation, practice your responses, and act in faith that this will make a difference. Then evaluate how it went. Make adjustments and try again. Be intentionally more positive with your children whatever their age.

Kids can get discouraged when their flaws are pointed out and then they are more likely to misbehave. Elder Neal A. Maxwell understood the power we have to choose how we will respond. Our children need us to choose wisely. "We can decide daily, or in an instant, in seemingly little things, whether we respond with a smile instead of a scowl, or whether we give warm praise instead of exhibiting icy indifference. Each response matters in its small moment. After all, moments are the molecules that make up eternity, affecting not only ourselves but others, because our conduct even in seemingly small things can be contagious."[34]

We have the power to choose how we will respond. We are also the ones that set the tone in our homes. Little things can add up and we can work towards creating a positive balance in our "accounts" with others by keeping things positive. Remember what we learn in Alma 37:6, "Now ye may suppose that this is foolishness in me; but behold I say unto you, that by small and simple things are great things brought to pass; and small means in many instances doth confound the wise."

"Speak kindly—say that which edifies. 'A soft answer turneth away wrath: but grievous words stir up anger' (Prov. 15:11). When we as parents avoid words that demean, tear down, disappoint, or discourage, we teach our children to avoid damaging habits. When we choose and use words that build, praise, compliment, uplift, and encourage, our children will be

---

34 Neal A. Maxwell, *The Promise of Discipleship*, (Salt Lake City: Deseret Book, 2001), 71.

motivated to do the same. They will thus be learning Christlike traits, and this behavior will help them feel good about themselves."[35]

Becoming More Consistently Positive

Constancy takes time and thought to achieve, but there are great blessings that come when we can act the same way regardless of what our children throw at us, literally or figuratively speaking. The more consistent we are, the more we are like Heavenly Father and Jesus Christ. Ponder the following quote and work to be more consistently kind, positive, and nurturing to others.

> The greatest example of all is the kindness displayed by our Heavenly Father and our Savior, Jesus Christ. Whenever I ponder their goodness, I envision kind, caring, and nurturing parents. I believe our Father constantly acts with love. Constancy is a characteristic of deity. Man is variable; Father is constant. Could we have faith in our Heavenly Father if He responded to our needs according to a mood? What if our blessings were contingent not on our behavior or on our Father's wisdom but on whether He was having a good or bad day? It would be impossible to develop strong, unshakable faith in such a being. But God is constant. We can go to our Heavenly Father in prayer, trusting that He loves us and that He truly understands our needs far better than we do. We know He will tutor us, guide us, and bless us in His kindly manner according to His knowledge and wisdom. If we desire to guide our children, bless the life of a spouse, or be worthy of a friend's confidence, we need to display more constant kindness. Then others may have trust in us, similar to the trust and faith we have in our Heavenly Father.
>
> There is much kindness in the world; every day many kind acts leave their marks on personal touchstones. Still, we know that one of our challenges here on earth is to develop godlike constancy in kindness. We must learn to respond consistently to life's ups and downs, acting with love and kindness regardless of challenges that lie in our path.[36]

---

35   Ronald L. Knighton, "Becoming Our Children's Greatest Teachers," *Ensign*, September 1999.

36   K. Richard Young, "Kindness: A Celestial Touchstone," *BYU Address*, November 1, 2005.

Intentional Positive Parenting

Workbook

Changing what we focus on and give attention to can change the atmosphere in our homes. The Savior was consistently positive with those around Him, and we can be like Him in this way. We can strive to build others up and avoid pointing out their flaws. Work through the *Intentionally Positive Parenting Workbook* to practice being a more positive parent, or discover your own ways to be consistently positive with your loved ones.

Positive Parenting Practice

1. How is Jesus positive with those around Him?

_____

_____

_____

_____

2. List the good things family members do daily. (Think big and small.)

_____

_____

_____

_____

Circle the positive behaviors you listed that you notice and acknowledge. Think about the good behaviors you are not acknowledging throughout your day. If we increase the positive things we notice, our family members are more likely to do them.

In the space below, practice making encouraging responses. Make a list of the positive things you observe your family members doing throughout the day and think of positive ways to acknowledge their efforts. By writing them out, you are more likely to acknowledge them when they happen. It helps to train our eyes to see the good around us.

1. Good Things I Can Notice:

_____

_____

_____

_____

2. Positive Responses I Could Give:

_____

_____

_____

_____

3. Evaluate your efforts. How do you feel about your efforts?

_____

_____

_____

_____

4. Did you feel closer to family members?

_____

_____

_____

_____

5. How did it feel to notice the good in others?

_____

_____

_____

_____

6. What was your family member's response to your efforts?

_____

_____

_____

_____

Challenge yourself to notice the good others around you are doing. See how many acknowledgments you can fit into your day. It doesn't cost you anything and it is simple to do. It can make a huge difference in shaping the behaviors of your family members. Study the Master, plan to be positive, act in His ways, and then reflect on your efforts, and pat yourself on the back for the improvements you are making.

Five Steps to Better Behavior[37]

1. *Teach Expectations*

   Children must often be taught, in very specific language, using examples and events drawn from their own lives, what it is they are expected to do, and how they are expected to behave. This is best taught through role-playing.

2. *Acknowledge appropriate behavior*

   A. Frequently (15-20 times per hour)
   B. Intermittently
   C. Casually/calmly/composed
   D. With brevity (taking only a few seconds and using few words)

---

37   Dr. Glenn L. Latham, "Five Steps to Better Behavior," *Utah State University Married Stake Fireside*, 1994.

E. Descriptively (use words that describe the behavior being reinforced)

3. *Apply Extinction*

Simply ignore (put into perspective) inconsequential, age-typical, annoying behaviors.

4. *Selectively reinforce the appropriate behaviors of others*

Be certain to have many positive interactions with children in the company of other children as they behave appropriately. These interactions should be

A. Pleasant
B. Brief (requiring only a few seconds and a few words)
C. Descriptive (use words that describe the behavior being reinforced)

5. *Stop, then redirect inappropriate behavior: then reinforce the appropriate behavior that follows*

It is not enough to simply stop a behavior. The behavior must be redirected, thus providing an opportunity to reinforce the appropriate, redirected behavior.

Remember: stop, redirect, reinforce.

Practice the Five Steps to Better Behavior

1. *Teach Expectations:* What behavior would you like to see go away? What is the behavior you would like to see instead?

_____

_____

_____

_____

Practice doing the new behavior with your child. (Have them practice putting their shoes in the basket by the door and explain this is what is expected of them and do it with a smile.)

2. *Acknowledge appropriate behavior:* What can you say to acknowledge the appropriate behavior?

_____

_____

_____

_____

Did you follow the suggestions for making these acknowledgments? Did you use fewer than ten words? (The goal is to be brief, especially if the child is young.)

_____

_____

_____

_____

3. *Apply Extinction:* Ignore the behavior you are trying to get rid of. Give your attention when they do the desired behavior. It really will be better to ignore the shoes in the wrong places!

_____

_____

_____

_____

4. *Selectively reinforce the appropriate behaviors of others:* How can you notice the appropriate behavior of your child?

_____

_____

_____

_____

5. *Stop, then redirect inappropriate behavior:* then reinforce the appropriate behavior that follows.

Most of the time the above steps are enough, but if your child continues to do the behavior they may need to have help. Stopping the behavior and then teaching them again (through role-play) will be helpful.

Positive Conversation Ideas with Children

From time to time, individuals get trapped in patterns of negativity that are hard to break. Siblings may make a habit of pointing out the flaws of other siblings. Parents and children both get stuck commenting for the sake of commenting. For many cultures, the comments are negative and cutting. Individuals feel the need to put down others in order to raise themselves up in front of the ones present in the room or on their social media platforms. This is not only a dangerous trend, but a very hard habit to break.

The following is a way to work one-on-one with an individual struggling with this. Read through the suggestions, and circle the numbered paragraphs you feel would work with your loved one. Like so many things in this book, this is only a suggestion. There are many ways to work through this issue. Pray for guidance, use this, or find your own way. Good luck!

1. Invite your family members to look at a "Highlights What's Wrong" picture. (Use the Internet to find one of these pictures. They have things out of place like square wheels on a bike, or a broom instead of a hockey stick.) Ask them to list the things that are wrong in the picture. (This works with children and adults alike.) Have fun with this! (Make sure you have some paper and pencils available. You will need them later.)

2. Say, "It is pretty easy to spot the things that are not right in this picture. Is the world really like this? Why or why not?" (Take responses and let them talk about this for a bit. Some may actually brag about how easy it was.)

3. Say, "Now I would like to challenge you to find the things that are right in the picture. (When they struggle, let them.) Compliment them for finding the good things they can see. Why is it so hard for us to see the good around us? Why is it so hard to see the good in our family members?" Let them respond. (Don't correct their thinking, just let them talk. It will amaze you what you can learn.)

4. Say, "It's hard to train our eyes to see the good around us, partially because there are so many good things to see that we get used to it and only see the

things that are out of place. It's hard to retrain our eyes to see the good. It is good we have the example of the Savior to help us.

5. Dallin H. Oaks said this about the Savior, "Our Savior, Jesus Christ, always builds us up and never tears us down."[38] How does He build us up? (Take responses.)

6. Can you picture the Savior saying kind things to the people around Him? Would He look for the good in others? Or would He say mean things?

7. Remind your children you rejoice because of them. List at least three things you love about your children and smile at them as you say them.

8. It's now time to give family members the tools they need to fix the problem. Express love and then move on to talking about the love you know they have for their sibling(s). Say, "Sometimes negative talk gets in the way of you showing your sibling/s that you love them. I would like you to think of the things you love about (name a sibling) and I'll write them down as you say them." (Or you could give them a piece of paper and let them write the things they like about their siblings). Give them an example and practice this with them before you set them loose with this task. Brainstorming sometimes takes time to get going, but once they get going, they can generate a lot of ideas. The longer they think about things, the better. You could write a list of your own about the child present or the one they are writing about. Let them tell you about their list. Be positive and excited about the things they list.

9. Say, "You have made an impressive list of things you love about your sibling. I'd like you to practice being positive like the Savior. See if you can say at least four positive things to your sibling today. The trick is to not say negative things to them. Try to only say one negative thing to them a day. If you get stuck, think about Jesus being positive with those around Him." A picture of the Savior could be given to them to remind them to try to be like Him.

People who are part of a family sometimes become overly critical of each other. ("You're going to wear that?", "You look awful today!", "You didn't pick up this or that!", "You stole my pants!", etc.) Some people get into the habit of being overly critical about things that don't really matter. This can ruin a relationship.

Another important aspect of avoiding being critical is learning to ignore taunts that get thrown at us by someone wanting to start a fight. These

38   Dallin H. Oaks, "The Atonement and Faith," *Ensign*, May 2010.

fights are often started out of boredom, habit, or because we don't know how to relate to people in any other way than to be critical. Role-playing how to ignore someone being critical of them helps others to know what to do. Practice saying nothing at all unless it is to thank someone, or to say something positive. Ignoring things that bug us is good practice no matter what relationship we are talking about.

Be positive about their attempts at being positive. This will work best if you look for times when they were positive and acknowledge their efforts. Smile, give them a thumbs up, or speak positive words. Be positive with them and then they will be more likely to be positive with others. Try to help them get to eight positive comments to every negative comment they utter. Kids like a good challenge when they have support from someone they love.

At the beginning of your child trying to be more positive, they will need lots of positive feedback. As time goes on and they get better at it, you can ease up on the frequency of your positive comments, but remember: the things you want to see need to be acknowledged.

Don't fall into the trap of catching them when they "mess up." If you need to step in because the hurt is great, it is best to let them figure out where they went wrong and offer support. ("I heard what was said after dinner. How did that make you feel?" Let them respond. "What do you think you need to do now?" Let them answer and offer them your support and confidence. "That sounds good. Words sometimes get away from us. I'm glad you're trying again. Let me know how it goes.")

"The eight-to-one rule has been related to a bank. You make deposits in your relationship bank when you make positive comments, and you make withdrawals when you make negative comments. Challenge kids to make deposits instead of withdrawals and check back with them often about the deposits they are making. This could be a fun way to check in with them using code words like deposits and withdrawals."[39]

Family Activity

Make a picture of a piggy bank and put it on a mason jar. Have family members write out things they did to make deposits in other people's banks and share them with the family during Family Council. Or you could have the person receiving the deposit write out the positive thing that was said to them. This is a fun way to encourage positive talk in the home.

---

39   Dr. Richard Young, Ward Fireside, given in Logan, Utah, November 13, 1994..

Positive Footsteps of Others

I was privileged to have two amazing bishops when I was a new mom. My husband and I benefited from their wise counsel. They seemed to know what tools young parents needed and did their best to teach us in a way we could learn. They were generous with their time and often had evening firesides where we could ask them anything about parenting. The following are some stories they told us, or used in books and talks they have written. These men helped me to change, and I wanted to share a bit of them with you. May these examples help you on your journey to follow Jesus Christ.

Recently I was in the front yard of a friend's home playing with my fifteen-month-old grandson. As fifteen-month-old babies do, he made a dash for the street. I gently picked him up, and said, "No, you may not play in the street." As I put him down on the sidewalk, I said, as I patted his back, "Play here," and I touched the ground. As expected, he headed right back for the street. Again, I gently picked him up and repeated the same corrective teaching strategy. After four learning trials, he went to the edge of the sidewalk, stopped, and looked up at me. I smiled, knelt down beside him, gave him a hug, and said, "Thank you for playing here," as I touched the ground. He went up and down the sidewalk for a few minutes, then, as to be expected, headed for the street. I repeated, word-for-word, action-for-action, exactly what I had done earlier. He played for a few minutes, headed for the street, stopped at the edge of the sidewalk, pointed to the street, and said, "No. Don't." Of course, that behavior was rewarded with a loving, tender consequence.

As we headed back into the house, I heard a terrible noise coming from next door. The child of the family living there, also about fifteen months old, went into the street. The boy's father screamed, "Get out of that street, you little brat!" while at the same time giving him a swat on the bottom and harshly putting the boy down on the lawn. The boy, by now, was crying in pain. You bet the boy didn't return to the street, nor did he seek out his father for comfort. My heart aches for that boy, but it aches even more for him and his entire family when he is fifteen years old. The child had been taught nothing about where he should play, but he was learning a lot about the distasteful effects of coercion, aversion, and pain.

As parents, we must not be seduced into believing that because we get immediate results from scolding, spanking, and screaming, these are appropriate ways to respond to inappropriate behavior. They are not. In the long run, behavior responds better to positive than negative consequences. Don't be blinded by immediate, short-lived results, or by immediate, short-lived gains. There is an economy in child-rearing, a price we must pay. Either we remain solvent with positives, or we are forever in debt and even bankrupted with negatives; positives that produce low-risk families or negatives that produce high-risk families.[40]

This is a story that Bishop Young told us that reminds us of the influence we can have on those around us:

When we act with kindness we radiate a special warmth and light that is godlike in its origin and nature. Mary Hill Peterson, a teacher of at-risk students in an inner-city junior high school, radiated such qualities. Mary, not a member of our faith, was a special colleague and friend. I observed her classroom often. On each occasion, I saw patient acts of kindness, genuine words of commendation, and sincere, honest praise expressed to every one of her students. It was obvious to everyone in the school that Mary was having a special effect on difficult students. One experience, in particular, illustrates this effect and her radiating qualities.

Early in the school year, Mary was approached after class by one of her students. He was a ninth-grade boy—unkempt in his appearance, failing in school, frequently disciplined for his inappropriate behavior, and probably involved in a local gang.

He spoke to Mrs. Peterson in a rude, disrespectful manner, saying (in more colorful language than I will use): "You're a phony. No one goes around praising others. People tell you how bad you are and that you do everything wrong. They don't praise you."

Mary paused for only a moment and then simply responded, "I know that not everyone compliments others, but a few years ago I decided that I didn't care what others did. I want to be the kind of person who looks for the good in others, finds it, and then praises them for it."

The student muttered some inappropriate remarks as he hurriedly left the room.

The significant part of the experience occurred several months later, in the spring. Again approaching his teacher privately after class, the student, this time very politely, remarked, "Mrs. Peterson, I just wanted to tell you that I have decided that I want to be like you."[41]

40   Dr. Glenn L. Latham, *The Power of Positive Parenting*, (Logan; P&T Ink, 1993),18.

41   K. Richard Young, *Kindness: A Celestial Touchstone*, BYU Address, November 1, 2005.

Chapter Six

Can Patience Be Learned?

The sound of chaos greeted Mike at his front door. He took a deep breath and said a quick prayer for patience, and then entered his home. His two daughters were in a tug-of-war match with an unopened cake mix. Mike's wife was changing a diaper blow-out, and the boys were chasing each other around the living room with their big outside Tonka trucks as mud flipped off the tires. Mike hadn't even been home for five minutes and his blood pressure was already rising.

Does this sound familiar? Does chaos reign supreme in your home? Are you constantly running low on patience because of the curve balls life seems to throw your way? Wouldn't it be nice if we could order patience on Amazon, and have it delivered? This may be a good use of drones. "Honey, your patience has arrived."

We live in a selfish world that teaches us to be centered on ourselves. Our tempers easily flare when someone takes too long in the line in front of us, or a child is reluctant to do what is asked of them. We think we are entitled to our rage because such and such "made" us angry. It's natural to be impatient, and Christlike to be patient. We can learn to leave our impatience behind and become more charitable, like Jesus, by taking the time to examine how to be patient.

In this chapter, we will explore how to develop more patience with our family members and ourselves. Patience is one of the key attributes we are trying to develop here on Earth. Being able to accept God's will and His timing can be challenging. We hope to face our challenges with patience and let our trials be for our good, but some days it's just tough. Developing the capacity to endure suffering, hardships, trouble, and opposition without becoming angry, anxious, or annoyed is not a simple thing. Patience takes a lifetime to figure out, and that is okay.

Jesus showed a great deal of patience during His mortal ministry. We see evidence of this throughout the scriptures as He interacted with many people. His patience was tested by the scribes and Pharisees, who tried to catch Him disobeying their interpretations of the Mosaic Laws. Some people were angry because He claimed to be the Son of God, and yet He stayed calm. Still, others crowded around Him hoping to truly know all that He could teach them. Some sought Him out to see miracles. Many of the situations He dealt with were difficult. We also face hard situations. Jesus understands our challenges. He can be an example to us even in the hard things we face as parents.

Jesus Acts Instead of Reacts to Difficult Situations

The key to Christ's ability to handle tricky situations during His mortal ministry was that He acted instead of reacted to the things that came His way. If Jesus had waited to decide how to act until the scribes and Pharisees brought the woman caught in adultery, He could have gotten into a shouting match with them, and then He would have lost the opportunity to heal and teach. Instead of reacting, He acted in such a way that promoted learning, understanding, and healing.

Patience is a big part of learning to act instead of reacting to the situations we face. We choose how we will act when a problem comes our way. We choose if we will remain patient or let our emotions get the better of us. Satan would like us to believe that we are victims to an emotion we can't control and that we are not responsible for our actions because someone or something "made" us mad. Satan wants us to miss the connection between anger and agency.[42]

It's hard not to lose our patience when we are surrounded by a raging storm like the one described at the beginning of this chapter. It's easy to be affected by the winds blowing around us. Preparing for possible storms before they happen helps us to weather them better.

Jesus didn't just decide to be patient and calm when problems arose. He took time to pray, reflect, ponder, and center Himself often. He was intentional in the way He lived His life. When Jesus woke in the morning, He didn't know what challenges He would face (at least I don't think He knew), but He could deliberately choose how He would respond. When we take

---

42   Robbins, 1998.

time to center ourselves, we will act with more purpose instead of reacting to the current conditions around us.

Christ's prayers to His Father prepared Him to face the challenges of His day. It takes patience to slow down and trust Heavenly Father, but when we do, things go better. Our prayers and intentional efforts to live more like Jesus will help us. It's like we are putting on our armor before we go into battle. Armor makes all the difference during the fight. Armor protects us from the fiery darts that come our way. As parents, we have many things thrown at us. Putting on our armor first thing in the morning safeguards us against being enticed to become angry or react negatively. Prayer arms us against these fiery darts.

I Just Wasn't Born with Patience

We may think being patient or impatient is just part of our personality or that we were just not "blessed" with patience. It's just the way we are. We can continue to say this, and we will probably lose our patience in the same way, day after day, week after week, and year after year. Or we can take a closer look at patience and learn better ways. Charity, the pure love of Christ, may give us the insight we need to develop patience.

Elder Robert C. Oaks helps us make this connection. He found that four of the thirteen elements of charity relate to patience (see Moroni 7:44-45). He points out the following,

> First, 'charity suffereth long.' That is what patience is all about. Charity 'is not easily provoked' is another aspect of this quality, as is charity 'beareth all things.' And finally, charity 'endureth all things' is certainly an expression of patience. From these defining elements it is evident that without patience gracing our soul, we would be seriously lacking with respect to a Christlike character.[43]

Parents are asked to suffer long and be kind. We also try to remain calm despite bearing many things. We do this because of the love we have for our family members. When we remain kind and calm, we are Christlike. Jesus shows us how to have charity and patience. The more we concentrate on how Jesus acted, the more we move toward being charitable.

Patience was something the Savior understood. He showed patience with His disciples despite their lack of faith and slowness in recognizing His divine mission. He didn't force anyone to follow Him but patiently

---

43   Robert C. Oaks, "The Power of Patience," *Ensign*, November 2006.

taught those around Him. Jesus gave people time to figure things out as they learned to walk in His footsteps.

A good example of Jesus giving someone time to work things out came after Christ's resurrection. Many of us have heard the expression "Doubting Thomas" and know it refers to Thomas, one of the original twelve apostles. Thomas said he would not believe Jesus was resurrected without seeing Jesus with his own eyes. Eight days later, Thomas and some of the other disciples were together when Jesus appeared again. Instead of being frustrated, Jesus lovingly showed Thomas the wounds in His hands and side and gave Thomas what he needed.[44] Jesus has this same love for all of us. He will patiently give us what we need.

Just like a toddler learning to walk, Jesus knew we would make mistakes, fall down, and sometimes need help up before we mastered walking. He is patient with us as we do this. We can be patient with our children as they learn to "walk" here on earth. Our patience gives our children safe places to land as they toddle along.

Jesus *Practiced* Being Patient

Jesus had many opportunities to practice being patient. We have discussed a few of those in this chapter. We can look at the events in the Savior's life that prepared Him for His ultimate test and realize He practiced being patient throughout His life. This practice helped Him face the ultimate test of patience. We are also given opportunities to practice being patient, but do we see it that way? Small moments give us a chance to practice being patient, which prepares us for the bigger tests we face.

We have chances to practice being patient every day, but sometimes we think we have to "save up" our patience for big things or important people. We may think, "I'll be calm when it really matters." We would never treat a coworker or an important client we are trying to impress with impatience. Our responses to our children are just as important, if not more so. So why do we "forget" to be patient with our children? They are the ones we are trying to impress the most while they are impressionable.

Jesus gave us the greatest examples of patience near the end of His life. His ability to endure trials was tested in Gethsemane. He endured unimaginable anguish as He atoned for our sins. In His agony, He didn't get angry. Instead, He uttered these words, ". . . O my Father, if it be possible, let this cup pass from me: nevertheless, not as I will, but as thou wilt."[45]

---

44   John 20:24-29.
45   Matthew 26:39.

Even in this moment, the Savior was learning how to be more patient with the sleeping disciples. The three times the Savior came out to talk to His disciples and feel of their love and support He found them sleeping. His first comment shows the desire He had for them to support Him. He seemed to gain more patience and compassion each time He came out to be with them. His acknowledgment and acceptance of how tired they were showed an increase in empathy and understanding. He put their needs before His own. His love for each of us comes through in His willingness to suffer and endure these hard things.

His patience was further tested when the Romans nailed Him to a cross where He would die, never murmuring a word of complaint, only offering forgiveness when He said, ". . . Father, forgive them; for they know not what they do."[46] He truly suffered, bore, and endured all things. His willingness to endure can inspire us to do hard things. Our hearts fill with joy and gratitude as we consider all that He has done for us. His courage can strengthen our resolve to be more patient.

We all have different challenges and struggles with patience. We will explore some of the challenges parents face to better understand them. Naming these challenges is the first step to overcoming them. Knowing we are not alone in our challenges can help us move forward.

How Do We Move Past Just Feeling Bad for Being Impatient?

Before we had kids, we may have pictured ourselves never yelling and never feeling frustrated, and then reality hit. Parenting is hard and challenges us in so many ways at once. We hate that we "lose it" with our kids, and feel guilty. Then we are hard on ourselves, and we curtail the yelling for a bit. But then we forget and yell again, or something new is thrown our way and then we feel guilty again. The cycle of yelling and feeling bad starts all over. We can get beyond just feeling bad about losing our patience, and use these feelings to help us change ourselves so we can get out of this cycle.

Repentance comes into play here and so does being charitable. Charity is not being easily provoked.[47] If we work at being slow to anger by repenting and coming up with a better plan to stay calm, things change in our relationships with family members. President Nelson helps us understand this, "When Jesus asks you and me to 'repent,' He is inviting us to change—our mind, our knowledge, our spirit—even the way we breathe. He is asking

---

46   Luke 23:34.
47   Moroni 7:45.

us to change the way we love, think, serve, spend our time, treat our wives, teach our children, and even care for our bodies."[48]

It appears daily repentance is about changing ourselves and not just turning away from sin. President Nelson suggests we change ourselves in some very real ways that may differ from what we currently view as repentance. This quote suggests we look at how we treat people, spend our time, and even care for our bodies. We can change the way we show love to our families by learning how to be more patient. When we focus on Jesus Christ, our hearts stay soft. We can see little things we can do to improve. We can work through issues without getting frustrated. By learning to be calm and patient with others, we learn to have power over ourselves.

Gaining mastery over ourselves feels so good. Doing hard things like controlling our tempers takes effort. The Lord knows this and loves when we make an effort to change. When we change even just a bit of ourselves to be more patient, the Lord helps us to find more happiness and joy because we've attempted to do and be better. Remember there is joy in daily repentance. When we work to control ourselves and stay calm and kind, we can feel joy. We can feel these benefits, but the real reward is seeing how our patience helps our home be a more loving, inviting place.

There is something to be said about remaining kind even when other people or situations are trying our patience. This is what one mom did to change something she struggled with. It was a pretty simple fix for a simple problem. She felt like she got after her son for annoying things that were harmless and just things kids do, so she found a way to be more patient.

> *My son loves to whistle. The only problem is that he whistles the same five notes repeatedly. I could handle the monotonous whistling most of the time, but sometimes I needed a break. If I had had enough, I would start a conversation with him or turn on the radio for a while, and then he wouldn't whistle, or he would whistle the song on the radio. I never had to say anything to him about his whistling and he even learned some new songs.*
> *- Amy Christensen, New Mexico, USA*

Can We Learn to Be More Patient?

Many of us doubt we can "learn" to be patient. It is just one of our weaknesses. That may be the case, but we know God can make our weaknesses strengths, if we humble ourselves.[49] When we humble ourselves before the

---

48   Russell M. Nelson, "We Can Do Better and Be Better," *Liahona*, May 2019.
49   Ether 12:27.

Lord, He can make our weak things strong. Being humble helps us to be teachable, and as a parent, we have a lot to learn. Parenting can be very humbling. Jesus Christ can be our best teacher if we let Him. He gave us many examples of patience. We can have faith in Him to help us be patient in our weaknesses until we are stronger.

Humbling ourselves and remembering His grace is sufficient to help us with our parenting dilemmas. Many of us choose to hold on to our guilt over our perceived shortcomings, and this impedes our ability to change. We get stuck in a cycle of guilt that is hard to break. If we reach out to the Lord, His grace will buoy us up. Jesus will tutor and guide us to be more patient. He loves us and wants us to succeed. It takes time and practice to become patient with ourselves and others, but His grace truly is sufficient.

Elder Dieter F. Uchtdorf reminds us, "Patience is a process of perfection. The Savior Himself said that in your patience you possess your souls. Or, to use another translation of the Greek text, in your patience you win mastery of your souls. Patience means to abide in faith, knowing that sometimes it is in the waiting rather than in the receiving that we grow the most. This was true in the time of the Savior. It is true in our time as well, for we are commanded in these latter days to 'continue in patience until ye are perfected.'"[50]

We can be patient with ourselves as we gain mastery over our souls. We inch toward being more complete when we work at being patient. Each time we stay calm during a stressful moment helps us on the road to be a more patient person. We can look to Jesus Christ. He is patient and kind. We can strive to be more like Him.

Family Councils Help Us Avoid Issues

If adding one more thing to your already busy schedule seems daunting, let me just say that adding family council once a week can save so much time. It has been worth the trouble in our family. It not only gave us a chance to connect with our family members, but we have avoided so many struggles by meeting together regularly. It also helps all family members be more patient because it gives us a forum to work through issues and a place to schedule and talk about upcoming events.

Elder M. Russell Ballard has written a great deal on councils. He said the following: "Please remember that a family council held regularly will help us spot family problems early and nip them in the bud; councils will give each family member a feeling of worth and importance; and most of all,

---

50   Dieter F. Uchtdorf, "Continue in Patience," *Ensign*, May 2010.

they will assist us to be more successful and happy in our precious relationships, within the walls of our homes."[51]

The family council meeting offers an ideal place where family members can resolve family problems and make family decisions. You can use (or not use) an agenda during the family council meetings. If you choose to use one, it can help you bring up touchy issues because it is not you bringing them up. It is being discussed because it is on the agenda. Placing a board where everyone can access and write items they would like to discuss sends the message that their needs are important. If the issue is resolved before the family council, they can cross it off but not erase it. We would still consult with those involved to confirm that the problem was solved to everyone's satisfaction.

Sometimes the biggest problem with having a family council is finding a time when family members can get together. Having it during or after Sunday dinner has worked for many. When children are small, having it during dinner might have some advantages. Young children may be less wiggly because they are occupied with eating. Meals tend to bring families together and happen at predictable times, so it wouldn't be hard to add family council to this time as long as you didn't do it before dinner. Hungry kids are less likely to be happy about having a meeting.

Family councils can come in different shapes and sizes and can be adjusted to the needs of the families and individuals involved. Family councils can be between a child and parents or include everyone in the family. It can happen over Zoom with extended family or in a variety of other ways. The goal is to help family members feel loved and understood. Children especially need to feel that others will listen to them. They need to feel connected to the family around them. Family councils provide a place for children to learn how to be a part of a group, and this can be a valuable tool.

Pep Talk

In Alma 17:10-12, the Lord gives the sons of Mosiah a little pep talk before they go on their missions. The Lord's words can help us take on the challenges of parenting. The Lord knows that parenting is tough. We can ask for the same comfort He gave the sons of Mosiah. We can go forth and do what the Lord asked us to do, and be an instrument in God's hands with our children. We can heed His promptings and take courage. The Lord asked the sons of Mosiah to be patient in their afflictions. He also asks us to be patient in ours. Preparing to be tested and tried helped these missionaries to be more patient.

---

51   "Family Councils," *Liahona* or *Ensign*, April 2016

Sometimes just knowing that we are going to be tested helps us face our parenting challenges and prepares us to be patient and our best selves.

We choose how we respond. President Nelson gave us a recent example of what motivated him to be patient. He was working with a surgeon who was so angry that he threw a scalpel, and it landed in President Nelson's forearm. President Nelson said the following about the incident, "This experience left a lasting impression on me. In that very hour, I promised myself that *whatever* happened in *my* operating room, I would *never* lose control of my emotions. I also vowed that day never to throw anything in anger—whether it be scalpels or words."[52] Deciding never to do something helps us when we face a difficult situation. Visualizing ourselves being in control helps us stay calm. President Nelson stayed calm, and we can choose to stay calm as well.

Learning Patience

When I was a kid, my mother had a cartoon cut out of the Sunday paper posted on our fridge. It reminded me not to complain about doing hard things (especially homework). It was a *Family Circle* cartoon that pictured young Billy sitting at the kitchen table with an open math book. The caption read, "I have so much homework tonight. It is going to take me at least three hours to complain about it." The question I always had was: did Billy ever get his homework done, or did he get stuck just complaining about his task?

Math has always been something I try to avoid, but I often found when I sat down to work through the problems, it wasn't so bad. Working out math problems on paper is kind of fun and actually takes less time than complaining about doing the work. Could this also be true about working through some of our problem spots with patience?

Sometimes we think everything is bad and we are doing everything wrong. We can get overwhelmed. Instead, we can look at our day and work to fix a trouble spot, and when that is fixed, we can move on to another spot. If we are intentional and work through some of our tricky spots when we are unemotional and in a good frame of mind, we can make some changes to our day and within ourselves that help us be more patient.

When I work on math problems, instead of just complaining about them, I find I can solve them pretty easily. I think we can take care of our parenting trouble spots similarly. We tend to waste our energy day after day complaining or dealing with the same problems in the same way and expecting different results.

---

52   Russell M. Nelson, "Peacemakers Needed," *Liahona*, May 2023.

It can feel so good to conquer a problem and find solutions to our daily struggles. Go to the workbook section of this chapter and roll up your sleeves to tackle a problem area. It will amaze you how good it feels. You may realize that it is not as bad as you thought. Looking at your problem areas gives you a chance to be intentional and act, instead of reacting to things that come your way. This gives you a chance to learn to be more patient, like the Savior.

Intentional Patience

Workbook

There are so many instances that give us glimpses of the Savior's patience. Jesus understood how to be patient. He acted instead of reacted to the people around Him. Think about His patience and reflect on His experiences. Ponder on the patience of the Savior throughout your day. When you have a quiet moment, write out your thoughts about the Lord's patience.

1. How would you describe His patience?

_____

_____

_____

_____

2. How did Jesus show patience to others? How is He patient with you?

_____

_____

_____

_____

3. When is it hard for you to be patient?

_____

_____

_____

_____

4. How can you be more like Him? Picture yourself having more Christlike patience.

_____

_____

_____

_____

5. How can you be more patient with yourself as you learn to be patient?

_____

_____

_____

_____

6. Can you concentrate on your positive attempts instead of the times you lack patience? Think about the Savior's patience and the love He has for you, and try to do likewise with yourself. How does knowing Heavenly Father and Jesus Christ will be patient with you help you be patient with yourself?

_____

_____

_____

_____

7. When can you show more Christlike patience during your day? Be specific. How will you let the Savior's example influence you today?

_____

_____

_____

_____

8. After you attempted to be more patient with a loved one or with yourself, how did you feel? How was it different from when you were impatient with yourself or others?

_____

_____

_____

_____

Patience is one of those things that takes a lifetime to develop. Every parent struggles with being patient in different circumstances. We all have different things that are hard for us. There are five areas we are going to spend some time on in the *Patient Parenting Workbook*. Other situations can try your patience, but we will concentrate on five common trouble spots so they don't trouble us anymore.

It's Hard to Stay Patient When. . .

1. Child/Teenager refuses to do as told.
2. Jobs are not completed in the specified time.
3. We have unmet personal needs.
4. Routines haven't been established to eliminate issues that try our patience.
5. Annoying behaviors of others get on our nerves. Are we dealing with the same bad behaviors at the same time every day?

Let's Practice

1. What should I do if my child/teen refuses to do what I ask them to do?

If we feel like our children are constantly refusing to do what we tell them to do and we are sounding like a broken record, try something new or change the record. We sometimes have the mistaken belief that we can keep doing the same things and get different results. It doesn't work that way. Let's walk through making a request so we can avoid problems with our children.

What is it that your child is refusing to do?

_____

_____

_____

_____

Teach them what is expected. Take the time to show them what you want them to do calmly. How will you do this? Remember, there is power in a polite request![53] If your child only responds when you yell, you have trained them to do this. Now it is time to teach them by using a polite request.

_____

_____

_____

_____

---

53   Poppin, 83.

Practice - Have your child practice what you need them to do. This is a very important step that often gets forgotten. Practicing a task sends the message you value what you are asking them to do. It helps both of you to know what the expectations are.

How did you and your child practice the task? Compliment them on doing the desired task. This is what I could say:

_____

_____

_____

_____

Show confidence in their ability to do the desired task.
I will show confidence in them by:

_____

_____

_____

_____

Check on them and give them another compliment.
The compliment I could give them is:

_____

_____

_____

_____

If they are still stuck, reteach them and then stay close by, but don't rescue them. Work alongside them on another task so you can have a pleasant conversation as the work gets done. Be positive about their efforts. Reteaching them the skill is not a punishment. Make sure you notice their attempts and be specific about your praise. Don't point out the things they did wrong. Give credit and recognize efforts.

If a power struggle develops over the chore, and the child is refusing to do the task, give your child a choice (not a threat). You can say something like, "I know this isn't your favorite job, but you are doing so well! You can choose to do it happily or be grumpy about it. Either way is fine with me (said without emotion). I hope you can get it done by seven p.m. so we have time to play a game of your choice." Then walk away. Let the consequences teach. If they complete the task in the designated time, enjoy a good game. If they didn't complete the task, you can say something like, "I like how you . . . but I'm afraid we don't have time for a game, though I was really looking forward to it. Let's work more quickly and get the job done next time so we have time for that game." Smile and just move on.

2. It is difficult to be patient when jobs are not completed in the specified time. Here are a few guidelines to help with this issue:

- Attach completion of jobs to something rewarding, like a family game. Make sure you don't rub it in too much that they don't get to participate. They will feel it without doing that. Let the consequences do the teaching for you.

- Set a timer and assign everyone a different job and see if you can beat the timer. If you do, celebrate in some fun way.

- Make sure your children know what is expected of them and that the task is something they can do successfully.

- Develop the philosophy, "Everybody works, then everybody plays." Then pick a time that everybody works, then everybody plays together afterward.

3. Is there a time of day when you lose your patience more easily?

Sometimes we need to look at the physical and emotional reasons we struggle to be patient. If we look at the time of day that is hard for us and pick it apart, we can sometimes see things we can change. Instead of dealing with the same hard things day after day, take a moment to be intentional with your efforts to be patient. See if you can change some things to make it easier to keep your cool. Ask yourself the following questions:

a. Is there a time of day when you lose your patience more easily than at other times? When is it?

_____

_____

_____

_____

b. Why do you think you lose your patience at this time of day?

_____

_____

_____

_____

c. Are you trying to do too many things during this time? If yes, what can you cut out?

_____

_____

_____

_____

d. Can you do anything earlier, during a less stressful time?

_____

_____

_____

_____

e. Are you trying to do too much and should have others help with the workload?

_____

_____

_____

_____

f. Are you distracted by a device, and then frustrated that you're being interrupted?

_____

_____

_____

g. Is the time stressful because of hunger? Maybe a healthy snack (for you and/or the kids) will make things go better.

_____

_____

_____

_____

Workbook Area

If you know this is a rough time of day for you, with a little planning you can change some things so that it is easier to be patient and calm.

4. Establish Routines—Establishing routines can help you be patient with others. Knowing what comes next has a calming effect on everyone.

Kids don't like to go to bed! It must be some unwritten rule. Did you know that establishing a nightly routine makes your job easier as a parent? It also helps your children feel safe and secure. How many of you have told your young son or daughter to go to bed and then ten minutes later you tell them to go to bed again? And then you yell at them again, and again, and you end up feeling frustrated, tired, and annoyed. Establishing a nightly routine helps you to avoid this headache.

The idea is to create a chain of events that mixes enjoyable things with things the child may dread. Look at the things that need to be done in the evening, and incorporate some fun and closeness into the end of every day.[54] Remember, blessings come when you stick to a plan that everyone can expect. If you already have a good bedtime routine, look for another time during the day a routine could make run more smoothly.

Routine	What Went Well?	What Needs to Change?

5. Are you dealing with the same inappropriate behaviors at the same time every day?

Ignore . . . Ignore . . . Ignore . . . Remember, the key to getting rid of inappropriate behaviors is to strengthen good behaviors and ignore the inappropriate behaviors. It really works. Choose to not be annoyed with inappropriate behaviors, and notice the good things others are doing. It sends the message that you give your attention to the good things being done.

Life can be challenging at times, and it takes a lot of patience to stay calm. Here are some situations that give you a chance to practice acting instead of reacting. Practice handling these situations as a disciple of Christ.

---

54   Michael H. Poplin, *Active Parenting: A Parent's Guide to Raising Happy and Successful Children*, 4th Edition, (Marietta, Active Parenting Publishers, 2014) 64-65.

1. Your daughter is learning how to ride her bike (or drive a car). How can you help her with this?

_____

_____

_____

_____

2. Your children are giggling and noisy at a restaurant. How can you exercise patience in this situation?

_____

_____

_____

_____

3. Your three-year-old child has a temper tantrum in the middle of a grocery store. How can you avoid yelling? How can you show patience?

_____

_____

_____

_____

4. Your teenager is struggling in school and needs help with his biology homework. How can you offer your support?

_____

_____

_____

_____

Chapter Seven

Jesus Is Joyful

The first steps of a baby are magical. Sharing in their joy as they teeter along is so much fun. Babies get so excited that their chubby little arms flap in the air and then their enthusiasm can cause them to fall over. My daughter, Natale, clapped her hands with joy as she learned to walk.

Creating a home where this and other joyful moments can take place is something we try to do. We hope to also create a safe place where there are soft places to land when they fall and make mistakes. We want our homes to be a place where all of our steps can become more sure as we gain confidence in following Jesus Christ.

We live in perilous times; and there seem to be dangers on every side. Many of us wonder how we can protect our loved ones (and ourselves) from all the commotion around us. Kevin J. Worthen, former BYU President, sheds some light on surviving today, he says, "Joy is the key to our spiritual survival in the trying times in which we live, as well as in the trying times that lie ahead of us. When we experience 'opposition, anxiety, heartache, pain, disappointment, and sorrow'—things all of us are likely to face in this coming year—how are we to survive? By tapping into the power of joy."[55] Did you notice this was said right before the pandemic started? Interesting.

According to President Worthen, we can survive and thrive today by tapping into joy. It seems a bit strange to do this as a survival mechanism, but think about it. We know that joy comes from focusing on Jesus Christ and His Plan of Happiness. The Lord blesses us to feel joy when we follow in His footsteps. This lets us know we are on the right track. President Nelson said, "The joy we feel has little to do with the circumstances of our lives and

---

55   Kevin J. Worthen, *Enduring Joy*, BYU Devotional, January 7, 2020.

everything to do with the focus of our lives."[56] When we focus on Jesus Christ, things change. Hearts, lives, situations . . . everything.

In 2 Corinthians 4:8-9, we learn, "We are troubled on every side, yet not distressed; we are perplexed, but not in despair; persecuted, but not forsaken; cast down, but not destroyed;" These things are made possible because our focus is on Jesus Christ. In short, seeking Jesus Christ, knowing Him, and following Him helps us create a place where love, peace, and joy can be found. Focusing on Jesus gives us the answers we seek.

In this book, we have sought the example of Jesus Christ in many aspects of parenting; and hopefully we have found solutions to everyday burdens that make our hearts heavy. We have sought answers to our deepest hurts and struggles. The more we seek to know Him, the more He can enter into our hearts to help us change. And we can find joy in the knowledge that we have sought Him.

Our gospel learning will fall flat if we just learn about Jesus Christ and don't apply that learning to our behavior and choices. Being well-versed in the scriptures so that we know the answers in Sunday School is not the end goal. Our goal is to be more like Jesus Christ. He exemplified the love our Father in Heaven has for us. Jesus walked perfectly here on earth. We can get overwhelmed by the thought of striving to be like Him, or we can take one step at a time and look to Him for the direction we should take. We truly can be perfected in Him.

The word "perfect" scares many. Some may think, "I'll never be perfect, so why bother!" That is not what our loving Heavenly Father wants for us. He wants us to be like His Son because He knows we can find joy in our attempts, and He knows this will make our time on earth easier. When we strive to follow Jesus Christ, even parenting can be easier.

One definition of the word "perfect" is complete, or fully developed. This definition may help us not get overwhelmed. Perfection seems hard to attain, but striving to be more complete is attainable. Striving more completely to love others, and more completely forgive others, can be done. Studying one attribute at a time gives us a place to start and can help us be more complete as we develop these characteristics more fully.

We can practice being more like Him during our interactions with our family members. We can strengthen our families in whatever season they are in because we are striving to intentionally apply Jesus Christ's teachings and attributes to our family life.

---

56   Russell M. Nelson, "Joy and Spiritual Survival," *Liahona*, November 2016.

In D&C 6:36, it reads, "Look unto me in every thought; doubt not, fear not." We truly can look to Him in all things. Even parenting. Or especially parenting. Our fears and doubts flee when we look to Him. President Nelson said the following, "Whatever questions or problems you have, the answer is always found in the life and teachings of Jesus Christ. Learn more about His Atonement, His love, His mercy, His doctrine, and His restored gospel of healing and progression. Turn to Him! Follow Him!"[57]

The answer is always Jesus Christ! "What would Jesus do?" is the right question to ask ourselves. This is not just for bracelets that teenagers wear. It's a wise question for all of us to ask ourselves. We can look to Christ with our parenting concerns. I know our concerns may seem large. Whether our children are two, twenty-two, or forty-two, it doesn't matter. We can get to know the Savior better so that when we have questions and concerns, we can ask ourselves, "What would Jesus do?" And because we know what He has done, His example can help us to know what to do. And if we don't know what He did, we can study His life until we do.

Some of you may be saying, "I can't possibly do this! I'm too flawed, and so is my family." The truth is we are ALL flawed, but not hopelessly flawed because of Jesus Christ. We don't have to do big things to feel joy. We can feel joy by doing small simple things. We just have to take the next right step. For instance, we can forgive someone that snapped at us, or be a good listener like Jesus was. Or we can stay calm when kids are fighting over pants. There's a story behind that last one.

A few years ago, as I studied the life of Jesus, I noticed that angry scribes and Pharisees had a lot in common with my angry teens, tweens, and tantrumming two-year-olds. (We had all three at once.) I decided to study how He dealt with them and then I had the following experience.

> It was just a typical busy Saturday morning at our house, but something felt a bit off, and I wondered what would erupt next. My sons were upset with each other because they had to clean their room. My girls had been bickering off and on all morning.
>
> I left the house for a minute to get a couple of groceries. On my return, before I even opened the kitchen door, I could hear a loud commotion. I took a steadying breath and said a quick prayer for patience before I opened the door. In the middle of our kitchen, my two daughters were literally in a tug-of-war fight over a pair of pants.
>
> Natale yelled, "These are my pants!"

57   Russell M. Nelson, "The Answer is Always Jesus Christ," *Liahona*, May 2023.

Janey responded, "Mom gave them to me because they are too small for you!" And then she tugged the pants toward herself.

No one had noticed my arrival. I gently put down my sack of groceries, and as I did so the youngest attempted to bring me into the argument, "Mom, these are my pants, aren't they?"

Natale piped in, "But Mom, they are my FAVORITE pants!"

Instead of answering right away, I started putting the groceries away. This made them both mad, and they yelled again. When they stopped yelling, I quietly said, "Looks like we've had a misunderstanding." And then I went back to my task.

On their third attempt to bring me into the argument I simply waited until they were quiet. One of them said, "Aren't you going to DO something?"

When they were quiet, I said, "I made a mistake. I passed the pants on and I didn't tell you. Sorry. I'll let you work this out, but know that if you determine the pants are too small, they will be replaced. Love you both. Let me know how you choose to work this out." I walked away as they looked on in stunned disbelief. A few minutes later, they came to me and calmly told me how they would handle their pants situation.

Staying calm has always been tough for me. When there are raised voices around me, I sometimes panic. Staying calm in this moment felt like a huge win for me. Looking to Jesus gave me direction and a new way to handle contentious moments. I had been studying the New Testament before this incident and reading about how Jesus dealt with some angry scribes and Pharisees who brought a woman who had been sinning to Him.[58] Jesus showed compassion to the woman, and didn't get into an argument with the contentious men. I tried to do this with my Pharisees! Oops, I mean daughters.

By taking time to breathe and picturing the Savior, I was able to stay in control. (I created a little wiggle room for myself.) Learning to act instead of react to the raised voices and obvious contention in the room was tough, but so worth it. My daughters' need for me to fix the mess did not mean I had to stoop to their level. I stayed above it by simply being quiet until they were ready to listen. They attempted to pull me into their argument three times and because I stayed calm, they calmed down. I could see both of their perspectives and was shown a way to deal with the situation. I realized that compassion and humility needed to rule my actions. Both girls felt they had been wronged. My quiet demeanor eased the contention. I felt so much joy in my heart after I dealt with this problem. It was indescribable.

---

58   John 8:2-12.

President Nelson understood this feeling and said, "The Savior offers peace that 'passeth all understanding,' He also offers an intensity, depth, and breadth of joy that defy human logic or mortal comprehension."[59] I experienced the peace and joy he talked about. I studied the Savior's example and then put it into action to solve a family problem. It felt so good knowing I had followed Jesus in this small way.

President Nelson explains an even deeper truth about joy. He said, "Joy is powerful, and focusing on joy brings God's power into our lives. As in all things, Jesus Christ is our ultimate exemplar, 'who for the joy that was set before Him endured the cross.' Think about that! In order for Him to endure the most excruciating experience ever endured on earth, our Savior focused on *joy!*"[60] Jesus focused on the joy He could bring to us by taking on our sins and making it possible for us to return to our Heavenly Parents. He thought about us! That is simply amazing!

Jesus can be an example to us and help us deal with small things like arguments over pants and big things like our eternal salvation. Joy and love were at the center of all He did. When we humbly ask ourselves, what Jesus would do, our lives change.

We may stumble and make missteps, but we can be gentle with ourselves and others because He is gentle with us. He recognizes our efforts and knows our hearts. He knows we will not walk perfectly the first time or the thirtieth time. Jesus will be there for us. He loves us and will not leave us. He will not forget us because we are written on His hands.[61]

The pants episode and other small victories I have had sustain me, bring me peace, and help me feel joy . . . true joy. I wish I could tell you I never make mistakes now that I understand this principle, but that is far from the truth! The difference is my mistakes don't devastate me because I trust that the Atonement of Jesus Christ gives me the ability to repent, move on, try again, and hopefully find joy. It buoys me up so I can do hard things and face my challenges with faith.

Your victories will look different than mine and they most likely will not be about pants, which is a recurring theme at our house. You can feel a measure of peace and joy knowing you followed the example of Jesus. This moment of victory over self will help motivate you to look to Him because you want to feel that way again. Joy is a powerful motivator and one worth pursuing.

---

59   Russell M. Nelson, "Joy and Spiritual Survival," *Ensign*, November 2016.
60   Russell M. Nelson, "Joy and Spiritual Survival," *Liahona*, November 2016.
61   1 Nephi 21:15-16.

We know that it is not easy to follow Jesus Christ. President Nelson said the following, "There is nothing easy or automatic about becoming such powerful disciples. Our focus must be riveted on the Savior and His gospel. It is mentally rigorous to strive to look unto Him in every thought. But when we do, our doubts and fears flee."[62]

The Lord will let you know you had a victory by giving you a feeling of peace and joy. This feeling lets you know you are on the right track. Take a moment to notice the feeling of joy so you can recognize it when you feel it again. Following Jesus Christ is where joy . . . true joy is found. Our children need to see us following Jesus Christ and finding joy. As things get more and more out of control in the world around us, it will help our family members to see our ability to find joy in following Jesus. It will reassure them He is the way and remind them that there is real safety in following Him. May our parenting efforts become more joyful because our focus is on Jesus Christ. He truly is the answer!

Intentional Joy
Workbook

Thinking about Joy

1. Remember a time you felt joy after solving a family problem, or solve a family problem in a more Christlike way and see how you feel afterward. Jot it down so that it is fresh in your memory. Describe it. Relive it. Hold on to it. Let it buoy you up.

_____

_____

_____

_____

---

62   Russell M. Nelson, "Drawing on the Powers of Heaven," *Ensign*, May 2017.

2. What do you need to do to feel that again?

_____

_____

_____

_____

3. Joy can be found in parenting when we follow Jesus Christ and try to develop Christlike attributes. What attribute would you like to work on now? Why?

_____

_____

_____

_____

4. Contemplate how it feels to know that Jesus relied on feeling joy to get through His time on the Cross. It sustained Him. How does this knowledge change you?

_____

_____

_____

_____

5. Think about the hard things you face. Will concentrating on joy help you get through them? Why?

_____

_____

_____

_____

6. What is the most impactful, life-changing thought you have had so far while reading this book? How can it help you in your parenting efforts?

_____

_____

_____

_____

7. What steps are you going to intentionally strive to take to parent in a more Christ-centered, intentional way?

_____

_____

_____

_____

Chapter Eight

Simon Becomes the Rock

Challenges come in all different shapes and sizes. Our daughter, Sydney, overcame a fear she had because her dad believed in her and gave her a chance to choose for herself if she would do something challenging.

We were living in England and eager to visit our first castle. Framlingham Castle had seen better days; the only thing left was the catwalk and the outer curtain of the castle. The catwalk skirted the entire top of the castle wall and provided a place we could walk around to enjoy the view or defend the castle from villainous foes, real or imagined. Over the centuries, small parts of the curtain wall had fallen. Wooden bridges had been placed over these sections of the catwalk and wall.

Sydney wasn't sure she wanted to cross these bridges because they were wooden and didn't seem as sturdy as the rest of the rock catwalk. Kerry didn't push her to cross these bridges. He told her when she was ready, she could try it. He showed her it was possible, but let it be her decision.

The view was breathtaking. We could see the whole surrounding countryside, and we had a wonderful view of the other parts of the castle. Sydney decided she wanted to see what was on the other side of the castle, but that meant she would have to cross some bridges. She decided she could try crossing the smallest bridge. She did this successfully and thought she could then try another bridge. Again, she was successful; and so she tried the biggest bridge. It was such a simple thing to work up to the biggest bridge.

Sometimes tasks seem too large, but we can break them down so children can be successful. I appreciated Kerry's calm approach to helping Sydney conquer her fears and this castle. He never forced her to cross the bridge or made her feel bad about being afraid. Sydney faced her fears because she was encouraged and not pushed.

Jesus knows how to encourage us to do hard things so we can reach our potential. We can be encouraging to those closest to us. In this chapter, we'll look at how Jesus encouraged Simon the Fisherman to become Peter the Rock.

How Did Simon, the Devoted, Courageous, Flawed Fisherman, Become Peter the Rock?

The Apostle Simon Peter was my boys' favorite ancient apostle when they were wee little lads. They loved his willingness to leave fishing behind to become a fisher of men. They insisted on being told the story of Peter walking on the water before they would go to sleep at night. His courage gave them the courage to do hard things.

Peter's plunge into the sea helped my boys get back up when they fell. We can all learn from Peter's flaws and his courage to overcome them. We see ourselves in Him. Peter was impulsive, impetuous, and often outspoken. He said things he would later regret, and sometimes spoke first and understood later. These flaws are our flaws. And yet the Savior saw something in him.

When Jesus started His earthly ministry, He could have chosen anyone to be His apostles. Jesus could have chosen the most learned of men, but He didn't. He chose a tax collector, a zealot, and flawed fishermen. Christ's selection was not based on their occupation or status in their community, but on their heart. Instead of focusing on their present weaknesses, Jesus concentrated on their future strengths and what He could help them become. Jesus saw potential. The Savior's encouragement helped Simon become the Rock.

In this chapter, we will look at how Peter and the other apostle's courage stemmed from Christ's belief in them. We can help our children have courage by believing in them. Let's spend some time with Simon Peter.

What's in a Name?

In John 1:42, we get a glimpse of what the Savior sees in Simon. It says the following: "And he (Andrew) brought him (Simon) to Jesus. And when Jesus beheld him, he said, Thou art Simon the son of Jona, thou shalt be called Cephas, which is by interpretation, A stone."

Could this name change signify that Jesus saw more in Simon? Perhaps. This may have been Christ's way of giving Simon something to reach for. The nickname Jesus gave Simon helped him become the rock that the church was built upon. It was like Jesus was saying, I know who you are, Simon. I know who your parents are, and I know who you can become. I see your willingness to learn, and your ability to be led by the Spirit. Good job! This name gave Simon Peter courage.

My bishop, Glenn Latham, gave my husband and me some wise advice when we were getting ready to name our oldest. He said, "It doesn't matter what you name your child as long as you attach good things to that name." Attaching good things to our children's names helps them feel good about themselves. It helps them have the courage to do hard things because they know someone believes in them. They feel that someone is seeing the good they are doing and not just concentrating on their mistakes.

Jesus did this for Peter. The nickname Jesus gave Simon helped him become the solid and firm leader who led the church after Jesus was no longer on Earth. Jesus believed in Peter and gave him a glimpse of this every time He called him Peter.

Jesus Encouraged Simon Peter

In Luke 5:1–10, Simon and his brothers had been fishing all night and hadn't caught anything. Not a single fish. Simon was discouraged and Jesus encouraged Simon Peter to try casting his nets on the other side of the boat. Simon Peter did as the Savior asked and he and his brothers caught so many fish their nets started breaking.

Our kids sometimes need to be encouraged to try something again. Kids may think that if they don't immediately have success, they never will. We can encourage our children to try again. We can also break tasks down into smaller bites that are easier to swallow, so our children are not over-whelmed. Jesus did this when He called the apostles to go on missions. He broke this task into smaller bites, so they knew what was expected of them.

Even though Peter and the other apostles' faith was still in its infancy, Jesus sent them on missions to demonstrate to them that He had faith in them and their ability to spread the good news of the gospel.[63] Jesus sent the message that He believed in them. He gave them the authority to act in His name. He was specific about what He asked these apostles to do. They were likely nervous about these missions, and felt overwhelmed. Knowing that Jesus had confidence in them, and that He was relying on them, helped the apostles to have courage to face their new responsibilities.

Responsibility is a refiner. When children are asked to do something just out of their comfort zone, they stretch and grow. Children learn new things

---

63   Matthew 10:1-15; Mark 6:7-13; Luke 9:1-6.

about themselves when they are being stretched. The early missions of the apostles refined them and helped them to rely on the Lord. Christ's confidence in them helped them to have the courage to rise above their challenges, which prepared them for future challenges. We can similarly prepare our children.

Jesus wanted to instill courage in His followers. Throughout the scriptures, we have examples of Him doing this. This was a small taste of how the Savior encouraged His followers. He wanted His disciples to continue following Him after He was no longer with them on earth. Jesus wanted His apostles to lead others in the way of truth and light. His followers were flawed and still learning themselves (just like us), but Jesus knew He could help them qualify for the work. He took every opportunity to teach and enlighten those around Him. Jesus knew His time was short and so sometimes His Apostles were tested and tried in some dramatic ways.

Peter's Courage Grew by Being Challenged

The account of Peter walking on the water[64] is an experience we can learn much from. It took courage for Peter to get out of the boat and step on the water. Peter did this because he was encouraged. Here's a look at his story:

Jesus and the apostles experienced several highs and lows in a short amount of time. They learned that John the Baptist had been killed, and even though Jesus needed time to mourn, He healed and served others who followed Him. He then had compassion on them and fed 5,000 people with a few loaves and fish. Later that evening, the apostles found themselves on the storm-tossed Sea of Galilee in a boat that wasn't making much progress. The apostles were probably tired of rowing and anxious when they spotted something coming towards them on the water. Just as they started to be afraid, Jesus called out to them. Peter then asks, ". . . Lord, if it be thou, bid me come unto thee on the water."[65]

Jesus simply says, "Come."[66] We can picture Peter getting out of the boat and, with eyes firmly fixed on the Savior, walking toward Him. In Peter's enthusiasm, did he take several steps without thinking about what he was doing? When Peter realized that he was on the water, it may have broken his concentration. With his eyes taking in the wind and the waves, Peter begins to sink. He calls out to Jesus to save him. Jesus immediately stretched forth His hand to help Peter. Jesus was there for him right away. After Jesus pulls him up, I picture the Savior embracing Peter to reassure him that he is okay.

---

64   Matthew 14:24-33.
65   Matthew 14:28.
66   Matthew 14:29.

This step out of the boat tested Peter's courage and his faith in the Savior. The miracles Peter witnessed Jesus perform and the interactions he'd had with Him helped Peter to have the courage to walk on water. Peter knew that with Jesus, miraculous things were possible.

Jesus then asks him, ". . . O thou of little faith, wherefore didst thou doubt?"[67] I have always thought it was like Jesus was saying, "Peter, you were doing so well. Why did you doubt?" Questioning Peter gives him a chance to think about why he started sinking. It may have given Peter time to reflect on what happened. Peter may have talked to Jesus about the fear he felt because of the winds and waves. Or that he doubted his ability to do this hard thing.

It may have sounded like Jesus was disappointed with Peter's lack of faith, but maybe not. Jesus may have been using this walk on the water as an informal evaluation, or a test to see how strong Peter's faith was and how much more he still needed to learn. Tests can strengthen our faith. In essence, Christ said, "Look at what you can do when you keep your eyes firmly fixed on me." Peter may have needed this well-timed question to help his roots sink deep. Peter is the one who has to believe in himself. Knowing that he walked on the water can help him be brave when he is challenged in the future.

Think about what happened after Peter sank into the water. We know that Jesus helped Peter get back up, but we don't know how they got back to the boat. I doubt that Jesus dragged Peter or that Peter crawled. I think it's likely they walked back to the boat arm in arm. I doubt that Jesus used this time to discourage Peter from ever doing something this hard again. I picture Jesus using this time to build Peter up, and help him understand that he can do hard things, being very understanding and encouraging as He did so. Jesus might have taught Peter that even when the winds and the waves are fierce, we can still carry on and do the work that needs to be done.

Jesus may have reminded Peter that he was chosen for this work and, even though he sank, he was still called by Jesus. This experience helped Peter to understand how others feel when they fall and how to help them get back up. Peter could help others get past their mistakes and move forward because he had fallen and needed help getting back up as well. Peter understood Jesus would walk with him even when the winds and waves were fierce. Peace is not found in the absence of storms, but in the presence of Jesus Christ, our Savior. Even when storms rage around us, we can have peace when we focus on Him. Jesus will walk with us in our darkest hours until the morning comes. We can find calm in Jesus Christ. Life is full of storms. Focus on Him and you will not sink.

---

67   Matthew 14:31.

This account gives us hope that God will help us when we have storms. We can help our children have the courage to face the challenges they have daily. By studying the Savior's encouraging example, we can better understand how to encourage our children. Being encouraging is something that can change lives. We can help our kids to get up. Our words and attitude can help them get back on their feet and try again. We can help them see that falling is part of learning. Mistakes happen, and we can learn from them. In this section, we will continue to look at ways to encourage others.

How Can I Be More Encouraging?

Let's go behind the scenes and talk about some things that help children have courage. Parents play a vital role in helping their children have courage. We want to encourage and not discourage our children. "The word courage comes from the French word 'Coeur' which means heart. Courage is the 'heart' or 'grit' that enables us to take risks for a known reason."[68]

Peter took a risk, and it helped him put his trust more firmly in the Savior. It is through risk-taking that we can develop characteristics like determination, obedience, trustworthiness . . . and whatever else we may strive for. Courage comes from believing in ourselves.[69] This is where Peter struggled, but because Jesus was encouraging, Peter could walk on the water. We can help our children do this as well in their "Walk on Water Moments." Our encouragement can make the impossible possible.

If we break the word "en-courage" into two parts, it means to "instill courage" or "instill heart."[70] So how do we instill courage in our children so they can face giants, dragons, and the kid next door? Peter's little walk gives us some important clues. Peter was willing to take this risk because he knew the Savior was there for him. Peter had past experiences with the Savior that built his confidence in his ability to follow the Savior. Peter also trusted Jesus and knew that if He believed Peter could walk on water, then it was possible.

Have you ever been with someone who believed in you? It just feels good to be around them because you know that in their eyes you are capable, confident, and have the necessary skills to succeed. Jesus feels this way about all of us. When I read the scriptures, I can sense His confidence and the love He has for all of us. His prophets and apostles also find ways to send us this message. He wants us to succeed and find joy. He believes in us and will guide our footsteps as we guide our children's steps.

---

68   Michael H. Popkin, *Active Parenting: A Parent's Guide to Raising Happy and Successful Children*, 4th Edition, (Marietta, Active Parenting Publishers, 2014), 109
69   Ibid.
70   Ibid, 118.

We want our children to have the courage to face challenges. Instilling courage or "heart" in our children doesn't have to be hard. Children like to have new experiences and they provide opportunities for us to challenge our kids. Go for a walk with them and cross a few bridges, or let them lead the way using a compass. Try ice skating, or shoot arrows. Let kids try new things in safe environments to build their courage. Being successful in one area can give them the courage to try other things. Learn to look for the things they do well rather than reminding them of their mistakes. Train your eyes to see the good, and share your positive view of them with them. These are such little things, but they can help kids have courage.

Train Our Eyes to See

I had an interesting experience watching *The Chosen*. I love the series, and seeing Christ's earthly ministry portrayed in such a realistic way is fascinating. I love how the disciples are portrayed as ordinary, flawed people who struggle with being boastful, headstrong, focused on the wrong things (like cinnamon cakes), and so many other relatable things. Seeing how Jesus enters their stories is life-changing.

Right before they portray Jesus giving the Sermon on the Mount, I remember thinking, "It is the end of Season Two, I thought we would see more growth in the disciples. They are still so flawed." It was just a passing thought, and then, when I watched the Sermon on the Mount episode, I realized the error of my ways. When Jesus is giving the sermon, there are flashbacks of the disciples exhibiting one of the beatitudes mentioned. It was like we were seeing the disciples through Christ's eyes. It was so powerful!

I was concentrating on their flaws, but Jesus focused on their strengths. Jesus is looking for our strengths and not our weaknesses (I mentioned this in Chapter 5). We can do this for our children. Life will be easier for them if they know someone believes in them and is looking for them to succeed. I am not suggesting we overdo this and contribute to an inflated sense of worth. Our goal is to foster confidence in their abilities without contributing to an inflated sense of self. If we are careful to base our positive comments on who they are becoming and their character, and not on awards and achievements, our children will be encouraged without getting a big ego.[71]

Janey is our youngest and takes a fair amount of teasing from her older siblings. Most of the teasing is fun and Janey enjoys it, but once in a while, their teasing gets to her. During a Christmas break when all the kids were home, we were playing games and some of the older siblings started teasing

---

71   Ibid, 112.

her about the whining she used to do. She took it for a while and then I could tell she had had enough. She looked at me and said, "Mom, tell them how I just get in and get jobs done without complaining." So I did. Instead of dwelling on past mistakes, she longed to be reminded of her growth. She needed someone to believe in her and see the good she was doing. We can do this for our kids. Training our eyes to notice the good is all it takes.

Overconfidence

Simon Peter relied on his strengths and was used to making his own decisions. Peter and the other apostles were grown men and used to doing things their own way. It must have been hard for them to learn to rely on the Lord instead of trusting solely in themselves. At times, their overconfidence was their downfall. Peter was humbled and kept in check with the Savior's gentle teachings and, at times, strong rebukes.

The apostles saw Jesus performing miracles, and they wanted to heal others as well. Peter would eventually lead the way in this.[72] He wanted to do all that Jesus did, but his faith and understanding needed further development. Sometimes Peter and the other apostles' enthusiasm outpaced their ability. We are all Simon wanting to become Peter. We have weaknesses and struggles, but if we let the Savior in, He can help us to become a rock.

Our kids might think their abilities are more than they are. They may be overconfident and risk being humbled. This can be a hard thing. We can be there to help them get back up if they fall. Overconfidence is part of the learning process. Learning what we can do takes practice. It is helpful to have someone there who believes in them. With help they will gain confidence in their abilities and learn to trust in what they can do, and not just what they think they can do.

Jesus helped Peter work through some of his overconfidence and learn to rely more on Jesus, and we can help our kids to get back up when they have been humbled because of their overconfidence.

Instilling Courage

Instilling courage in our children helps them believe they can do many things. Here are a few simple ways we can send them the message that they are capable. We can build them up by focusing on what they do well instead of focusing on their mistakes. It is a real temptation to point out flaws, but doing so may discourage children. Instead, we can catch them "doin' somethin' good." "Wow, you've completed half of your assignment! You have

---

72   Acts 3:1-9.

worked hard! Keep going!" or "Thanks for getting the dishes washed. I appreciate it!" By giving credit and recognizing the efforts they are making, we build their courage. They need this from us. It goes a long way in helping them feel noticed and appreciated.

We all need to be noticed for the things we contribute. Saying things like, "I saw you smile at your little sister" or "I noticed you remembered to scoot in your chair. Thank you!" lets others know we see them. In essence, this is a way of saying, "I notice you! I see the efforts you are making."

Our children see us doing so many things and wonder if they will ever be able to do similarly. Kids oftentimes have more enthusiasm than skill. Being patient and finding tasks they are capable of doing builds their self-esteem. Kids like to help and be a part of family jobs. Two- and three-year-olds love to clean (Twelve- and thirteen-year-olds not so much). They love to sweep, dust, and do anything they see their parents or siblings doing. They may not do it up to our standards, but letting them feel useful and needed is valuable.

Encouraging others doesn't cost us anything, and it is easy to do. Our support and love can stay with our children for a lifetime. Choosing words that build and uplift is something we can do every day. The following is a wonderful example of the lasting effects of encouragement. Elder Joseph B. Wirthlin said,

> Kind words not only lift our spirits in the moment they are given, but they can linger with us over the years. One day, when I was in college, a man seven years my senior congratulated me on my performance in a football game. He not only praised how well I had done in the game, but he had noticed that I had shown good sportsmanship. Even though this conversation happened more than sixty years ago, and even though it's highly unlikely the person who complimented me has any recollection of this conversation, I still remember the kind words spoken to me that day by Gordon B. Hinckley, who would later become President of the Church.[73]

It is amazing how long these words stayed with Elder Wirthlin. Can you remember any of the kind words others have said to you? Why do you think you can still remember these encouraging words? What meaningful words of encouragement could you give your children?

Our encouraging words can stay with our children. In the workbook portion of this chapter, you will have an opportunity to write a letter of encouragement to your children. I hope you will write one. I still pull out encouraging letters friends and family have written to me when I need a boost.

---

73   Joseph B. Wirthlin, "The Virtue of Kindness," *Ensign*, April 2005.

What Do I Do after a "Walk on Water Moment?"

Simon Peter's "Walk on Water" moment helped him to become Peter the Rock. He learned so much from the experience, but we miss so much if we just focus on when Peter sank. He doesn't need to be remembered as the apostle who sunk, but as the man who relied on the Lord and got back up to try again. Peter firmly fixed his eyes on the Savior and made it back to the boat walking on the storm-tossed sea. Jesus walked side by side with Peter as the winds and waves crashed around them. This helped transform him into the rock he needed to be.

How can we make the moments our children sink into transformative moments that strengthen and encourage them to try again? How can we help them get back up after they sink? Here are some things to keep in mind:

1. Encourage them to try again.
2. Cheer them on.
3. Help them up if they fall. (Jesus was there for Peter and helped him get up).
4. Remind them of what they were able to accomplish. Be a positive voice reminding them of their successes as you dust off their knees.
5. Help them work through why they fell. Ask them why they think they fell. Be prepared for emotions, and for them to look for someone or something else to blame. Even if there was blame somewhere else, help them to concentrate on what they could do differently next time.
6. Concentrate on their progress. After you have examined why they fell, put the focus on the progress they made and prepare them to succeed in the future.
7. Try again. If possible, give them a chance to get back on the horse again.

We sometimes have the mistaken belief that we always have to find something kids need to improve upon to help them grow. This is fine, but another approach we can use is to watch for the things that go well and talk about those moments. This may help them focus on their successes instead of dwelling on the times they fall.

My daughter Natale loves volleyball and she would sometimes get discouraged because she didn't get more points for her team or she missed some serves. Kerry would ask her questions about plays that went well. He would ask her how it felt to get the kill in the second game or how the momentum shifted for the better after she talked to her teammates during a time-out. He found ways to let her talk about the things that went well instead of dwelling on her missteps. We still talked about the missteps, but it wasn't what we focused on. That way she went away recharged instead of being weighed down by mistakes.

This was his way of helping her up when she was down. He reminded her of what went well and helped her have perspective on her lows in the game. He noticed how after she missed the ball in the third game; the setter ran the same play, and she got it that time. By asking her how it felt to nail it, she shared a triumphant moment with us. Kerry didn't try to impress her with his volleyball knowledge or fill her head with all of her mistakes. He asked questions and got her talking about the game. Encouraging our kids is something we can do to help them have courage.

Peter did hard things because of the Savior's encouragement and love. Peter's faith did not waiver as he led the church after the Savior's earthly ministry was done. Peter had the faith and courage to heal a man outside the temple and perform other miracles (Acts 3:1-9). He bore powerful testimony of the Savior and organized and ran the church because he knew Jesus believed in his ability to do these things. Peter's faith was solid because while Peter was learning, Jesus was there to encourage him and help him back on his feet when he needed help. Jesus gave Simon a vision of who he could become and through His encouragement, Peter became the Rock.

Intentional Encouragement
Workbook

Letter of Encouragement

Writing children an encouraging note is a great way to practice using your new skills. The Savior is encouraging, and we can be like Him with our children. Life is hard, but if children know their parents believe in them, hard things are more bearable. Write a letter of encouragement to your child/children. It will mean a lot to them.

Putting words down on paper gives tangible proof of our love and belief in them. A good example of the power of giving our children tangible proof of the feelings we have for them was talked about in the October 2023 General Conference. Sister Runia spoke about the letters her father wrote to her. She said the following, "I went through a rough patch my senior year in high school when I wasn't making great choices. I remember seeing my mom crying, and I wondered if I'd disappointed her. At the time, I worried that her tears meant she'd lost hope for me, and if she didn't feel hope for me, maybe there wasn't a way back.

But my dad was more practiced at zooming out and taking the long view. He'd learned from experience that worry feels a lot like love, but it's not the same. He used the eye of faith to see that everything would work out, and his hopeful approach changed me.

When I graduated from high school and went to BYU, my dad sent letters reminding me of who I was. He became my cheerleader, and everybody needs a cheerleader—someone who isn't telling you, "You're not running fast enough"; they're lovingly reminding you that you can[74].

We can be a cheerleader for our kids. We can remind them of who they are and notice who they are trying to become. We don't have to say they have improved if they haven't, but we can see the efforts they are making and the things they are trying to accomplish. We can be specific with our words and see the good in them. We don't have to wait for special occasions to write them notes of encouragement, but birthdays and the beginning and end of school years are natural times to do this.

When kids get discouraged, they don't see things clearly. Give them a positive glimpse of how you view them. It may surprise them how you feel. It may counter the discouraging thoughts they have about themselves or the unkind words others have said. Writing an old-fashioned handwritten note gives them a boost when they need it and can be a priceless treasure for years to come.

Practice in Being Encouraging

1. What things are your children trying to accomplish right now?

_____

_____

_____

_____

---

74   Tamara W. Runia, "Seeing God's Family through the Overview Lens," *Liahona*, October 2023.

2. How can you support them in their efforts? How can you show confidence in their abilities?

_____

_____

_____

_____

3. Has the task been broken into small enough chunks?

Yes _____ No_____

4. If you answer "No," break the task up into smaller, easily accomplished chunks appropriate for the age and ability of your child.

_____

_____

5. What past successes has your child had that you can remind them of to help them succeed with their current challenge?

_____

_____

6. What words of encouragement can you say to your child?

_____

_____

_____

_____

7. What other ways can you send the message you believe in them? Example: Watch them participate in a sporting event, smile at them, etc.

_____

_____

_____

_____

8. In what ways are you concentrating on improvement, instead of perfection?

_____

_____

_____

_____

9. How are you concentrating on stimulating independence?

_____

_____

_____

_____

10. How did your children respond to your efforts of being encouraging?

_____

_____

_____

_____

Teaching Children Values

We want our children to be good humans. We want them to be honest, true, chaste, benevolent, virtuous, and to do good to all men. We want them to have the courage to exhibit these values that seem to be lost in our troubled world. How do we help them have these character traits? The Thirteenth Article of Faith gives us some clues. It says,

> We believe in being honest, true, chaste, benevolent, virtuous, and in doing good to all men; indeed, we may say that we follow the admonition of Paul—We believe all things, we hope all things, we have endured many things, and hope to be able to endure all things. If there is anything virtuous, lovely, or of good report or praiseworthy, we seek after these things.[75]

This Article of Faith gives us a glimpse of the things we believe in and seek after. The last line of this Article of Faith gives us guidance on what we can seek after in our children. We can look for the virtuous, lovely, and praiseworthy things in them. By becoming a "noticer," we encourage our children. By noticing the good, we are more able to encourage them.

The following walks you through teaching children values in a way that is easy to accomplish. Sometimes we want to make this more difficult than it needs to be. We think we need to have formal lessons on these virtues, but it can be much simpler than that. As we go about our normal lives, we can watch for our kids to be honest, kind, trustworthy, etc. By simply acknowledging their efforts, we send the message that these things are important to us. We don't need to make this more complicated than it is. We just need to watch for these traits in our children and "catch 'em bein' good."

Teaching Your Children Important Character Traits and Values

1. Make a list of the character traits and values you want your children to have.
2. Put the list in a place where you will see it often. (Mine was inside the medicine cabinet, and I looked at it when I brushed my teeth.)
3. Look for these traits in your children. When you see your children exhibiting these traits or values, let them know you noticed them. Acknowledge the traits you want to see more of. Example: You're

---

75   Article of Faith 13.

playing a game, and a child is close to winning, but someone else beats him to the finish and he was a good sport about it. Parent: *"Wow, you were so close. I bet that was tough not winning. Thanks for being a good sport."*

4. Look for these traits in others you come in contact with. Simply point out someone who is kind when they are being kind, or notice someone being honest when you see honesty. Being a noticer helps your kids to notice the good in others as well. Training our eyes to see the good around us is such an important skill. There really is a lot to see.

5. Ignore the times they are not exhibiting the traits you would like to see. Don't use your attention to reward behaviors you don't want to see again.

But What if You Can't Ignore a Behavior?

If you see a behavior that you just can't ignore, and feel that you need to address it, talk to your child in private and ask them how they felt when they acted in a way that was not consistent with your family values. See what they say and let the Spirit guide you in how you respond. If we are patient, we can teach lessons that encourage the characteristics we want to see. The following is what I did when my daughter was dishonest.

We were playing games as a family and having a great time, but then my daughter got caught cheating by her brother. She was embarrassed, but he was kind about his discovery. She tried to cover up her mistake, but we all knew that she had cheated. That night I didn't sleep well. One reason our family plays games is to help our children learn how to be honest. I didn't want to handle this wrong. I knew talking to her about it shouldn't be done in front of the other children, but I wanted to help her with this while it was a small problem.

The next day, when she and I were cleaning the kitchen, I asked her how she felt when she cheated. She said she felt horrible. Her eyes were full of tears. I hugged her and we talked for a bit about her feelings and how it was the Holy Ghost's way of letting her know cheating was wrong. We talked about winning and being competitive. I didn't overdo it and let her do most of the talking.

Now when we play games, she has been trying to be honest and a better sport. I thank her in private for her efforts and let her tell me about how happy her heart feels when she resists the temptation to cheat. She is improving and is a joy to be around as we play games. I'm glad we can move past this and that her siblings gave her another chance to learn to be honest.

We can gently lead our children to be more honest by questioning them about how they feel. We don't have to berate them for being dishonest, or yell at them. When we listen, we have a better chance to teach. Gentle questions are how the Savior often helped people to understand important ideas by helping them to understand themselves a bit better. He did this by listening to them. We can encourage honesty and give our children safe places to practice.

When we have behaviors we just can't ignore, here is something to consider. Dr. Latham said that many parents use D&C 121:43 to justify yelling and berating their children when they do something wrong. It reads, "Reproving betimes with sharpness, when moved upon by the Holy Ghost; and then showing forth afterwards an increase of love toward him whom thou hast reproved, lest he esteem thee to be his enemy." These parents miss the part about an increase of love toward the one that has been reproved.

I thank my bishop, Dr. Latham, for pointing out that according to Webster's Dictionary "reprove" means to correct, usually gently or with kindly intent, and "sharpness" means clear in outline or detail, set forth with clarity and distinctness. "Sharpness" can also mean directness. These definitions clarify what the Lord was saying. When we correct with gentleness and directness, being led by the Holy Ghost, behaviors and attitudes can change, especially when we show an increase of love afterward when we see their efforts to improve.

There were times that Jesus reproved with sharpness. The direct questions Jesus asked others led them to change. After Peter sunk in the depths of the sea and Jesus lifted him up, Jesus asked him, ". . . O thou of little faith, wherefore didst thou doubt?"[76] We discussed earlier what this discussion may have looked like. Peter's walk on the water changed him and helped him to become the rock that led the primitive church through a difficult time. Peter did not waiver. (Well, we have record of him denying Christ three times, but after that, he did not waiver.) All of these things gave him experience and strengthened him. He learned to trust the Lord, to follow Him, and to believe in himself. He learned he was capable of what he was being asked to do because Jesus believed in Him. We can do likewise.

---

76   Matthew 14:31.

Practice Being Encouraging After a Mistake

1. What could you say to a child after they made a mistake? How can you encourage them to try again?

_____

_____

_____

_____

2. How could you talk to a child who said something unkind to a sibling or friend? How would asking them how they felt when they said the unkind thing help you to teach them about the way the Holy Ghost helps us to know right from wrong? How could you encourage them to be kind?

_____

_____

_____

_____

3. How could you encourage your twenty-year-old who wants to quit college? How can your listening skills help you be encouraging?

_____

_____

_____

_____

Chapter Nine

Jesus Heals, and So Can We

What Should I Do?

Thory came home for the third day in a row with the weight of the world on his shoulders. Third-graders shouldn't carry this type of load. He sat down at the kitchen table to eat a snack. Usually Thory talked a mile a minute, but today he was pretty quiet. I decided to do some digging.

"So. . . how was school?"

"Fine," Thory said as he dunked his Oreo in milk. Having Oreos was a treat, and it usually made him smile, but not today.

I tried again. "It doesn't seem like it was fine."

Thory sighed and then said, "I fought with John again today. He keeps changing the rules in the game we're playing, and it was so annoying."

"I'm sorry. That sounds frustrating," I said. In my head, I was frantically searching for the right words to ease his burden. He was so discouraged.

What was I supposed to do?

It's hard to know how to help a loved one when they are carrying heavy burdens. Thory's burden was light compared to what some children face, but in his world on that day, it felt heavy. When my children started school, I found my role shifting. My kids were capable of so much more than they had been before, but they often needed help unraveling their next step. Sometimes they needed more than a listening ear, and other times that was all it took. Knowing what role I should play in helping them solve problems was tricky.

Looking to the Savior for direction in this can help us ease burdens and help our children heal.

Helping Others to Heal

One thing Jesus was widely known for when He walked on this earth was His ability to heal. People spoke of the miracles He performed far and wide. He healed the sick, caused the blind to see, cleansed lepers, forgave sin, healed broken hearts, and even raised people from the dead. His ministry was defined by the miracles He performed. How can we ever hope to be like Him in this way? What can we learn about parenting from the times He healed others?

As parents, we are also called upon to do many things to help our children heal and work through challenges. Parents tend the sick, heal broken hearts, forgive others of their trespasses, nurture those in need, and help them work through issues that arise (like trouble with friends). These things allow us to be His hands here on earth. We can practice being more like Him when we offer our family members our love and support.

Parents may find themselves walking a fine line between doing too much for their kids and not doing enough to support them where they are developmentally. It is hard to know how much we should do for our children or whether we should stand back and let them spread their wings and fly. Should we step in and fix a problem they are having with a sibling, or let them work it out on their own? If they are having trouble getting along with a friend at school, should we step in and help them or let them solve it by themselves? It's hard to know when to step in, or if we should just play a supporting role.

We have to be careful with how much we take on. We are actually trying to work ourselves out of a job. When our children are small, they depend on us for everything, but as they age, they start taking on more and more responsibility until they are capable of caring for themselves. As they are growing up, we have to be constantly evaluating how much we will do for our children and how much they are capable of doing for themselves. We should avoid doing something for our children that they are capable of doing for themselves. The trick is learning what role we play with our children when problems arise.

Look at the following three accounts of the Savior healing those in need to give us insight into ways we can be His hands with our loved ones. We'll look at the role Jesus played in these healings. Not only did He relieve suffering, but He let individuals do as much as they possibly could. These faithful people played a part in their own healing. We can follow Christ's example with our sons and daughters.

Jesus Removed the Burdens of Mary Magdalene

Jesus cast out seven devils from Mary Magdalene.[77] Mary could not remove the evil spirits from herself. This was a heavy burden and one she needed help with. We can only imagine how hard her life might have been before Jesus helped her find relief. We know little about how Jesus did this, but we know she became a faithful disciple of the Savior. After she was healed, Mary followed Him as He went about teaching. She was there when He was on the Cross,[78] and she stayed near the tomb where His body was placed.[79] She was the one who first spoke to the resurrected Savior.[80] His healing touch forever changed her life.

When we ease the burdens of others, hearts are changed and softened. Relationships can be strengthened and healed. We can be there for our children in a similar way as Jesus was for Mary Magdalene. Sometimes our children need us to remove the heavy burden they are carrying.

Jesus Helped the Blind Man See

In John 9:1-41, Jesus healed a blind man by putting mud on his eyes. Then Jesus instructed him to wash in the pool of Siloam. This blind man had the faith to go to this pool and wash off his eyes, and he was healed. Jesus did not do everything for him; the man had to do some things on his own. His faith fueled him to go to the pool, which he was capable of doing. Jesus gave this man the opportunity to have a part in his healing. Jesus understood what the man could do for himself and what he needed help with.

Jesus Supported Someone's Effort to Be Healed

We have one more stop-off in Capernaum before we tie these three miracles together. This miracle took place on the busy streets and forever changed the life of one woman who had been suffering for twelve years. Here's a recap of her story:

Jarius, a ruler of the synagogue in Capernaum, had just come to the Savior and asked Jesus to help his daughter, who was really sick.[81] Jarius was an important person in the community. Jesus went with Jarius to his house. As they were walking through the busy streets of Capernaum, Jesus

---

77   Luke 8:2.
78   Matthew 27:56; Mark 15:40; John 19:25.
79   Matthew 28:1; Mark 16:1, Luke 24:10; John 20:1,11.
80   Mark 16:9; John 20:14-18.
81   Mark 5:21-24, 35-43.

felt someone touch His robe and felt virtue leave Him.[82] Jesus could have overlooked the woman because someone "important" needed His help. But Jesus took time for this woman. She was not only healed physically, but His kindness and attention healed her forgotten spirit as well.

Each of the healings Jesus performed was personal. He healed people one by one, and knew what their needs were. People came to the Savior for help with their problems. They came with various maladies, and asked the Savior to heal them. He chose the role He would play in their healing, just as we choose how we will help our children when they come to us with their problems. Sometimes Jesus removed the burden from the individual because it was too much for them to bear alone. Mary Magdalene could not help herself and needed His healing grace to be rid of the evil spirits that possessed her. When Jesus healed the blind man, He placed mud on the blind man's eyes, and then, in faith, the blind man washed the mud from his eyes and was healed. His walk to the pool of Siloam was part of his healing; and this walk helped his faith to grow. The woman with an issue of blood had a plan and just needed to touch His garment to be healed. Her faith made her whole.

We want our children to be whole and capable of handling the challenges they face in their lives. When they are young and learning how to navigate life on this earth, we are there to guide and support them (and encourage them like we learned in the last chapter).

As parents, we are often given opportunities to be the Savior's hands. Our children bring their dilemmas to us. Sometimes they need us to solve the problem, other times they need someone to share their burden so they can face their trial. Other times, they just need to tell someone how they solved a problem so they can get feedback on how they did. We can offer healing to our family members day-to-day, and offer our support in their hour of need. The Savior is an example to us of how to play these roles.

President Hinckley said the following about the Savior's role as a healer:

Jesus of Nazareth healed the sick among whom He moved. His regenerating power is with us today to be invoked through His holy priesthood. His divine teachings, His incomparable example, His matchless life, His all-encompassing sacrifice will bring healing to broken hearts, reconciliation to those who argue and shout, even peace to nations if sought with humility and forgiveness and love.

As members of the Church of Jesus Christ, ours is a ministry of healing, with a duty to bind the wounds and ease the pain of those who suffer. Upon a world afflicted with greed and contention, upon

---

82   Mark 5:30.

families distressed by argument and selfishness, upon individuals burdened with sin and troubles and sorrows, I invoke the healing power of Christ, giving my witness of its efficacy and wonder. I testify of Him who is the great source of healing. He is the Son of God, the Redeemer of the world, 'The Son of Righteousness,' who came 'with healing in his wings.' Of this, I humbly testify in the name of the Lord Jesus Christ, amen.[83]

Parenting Helps for Healing

One of the realities of life is that we all face problems. These problems allow us to learn and grow. Parents want to help their children face their challenges and make good decisions. We want the best for our children. We don't like to see them sad, in pain, or frustrated. Our instincts may be to jump in and rescue our kids from whatever conflict or problem they are having. We know what it feels like to be treated unfairly or be picked on, and we want to help. If we jump in and rescue them every time they have a problem, will they learn to handle things on their own? Will they grow?

Back to our situation from the beginning of this chapter: I wanted to jump in and rescue Thory from his argument with John, but this would not have helped him. As we talked more about the situation, Thory decided that he and his friends were too grown up to play imagination games anymore. I encouraged him to play games with established rules like basketball and four square. John liked the idea when Thory talked to him, and they went on to continue to have fun at recess. It ended up being a pretty simple fix. Thory went back to enjoying his Oreos and other snacks much more after that.

There are times when parents should step in and relieve burdens, but so often, our role is to support our children as they solve problems big and small. If we hope to help them face their challenges, the first question we should ask ourselves is, "Who owns the problem?" Dr. Micheal H. Popkin, creator of Active Parenting stresses the need for parents to figure out who owns the problem before it can be solved. Here are some guidelines he gives for figuring out our role:

1. Who is the problem behavior directly affecting? Whose needs or goals are being blocked? Who is raising the issue or making the complaint? That person usually owns the problem.
2. Does the problem involve health, safety, or family rules, or values? If so, then the problem belongs to the parent.

---

83   Gordon B. Hinckley, "The Healing Power of Christ," *Ensign*, October 1988.

3. Is the problem within reasonable limits for your child's age and level of maturity? If not, then either the parent owns the problem or it is shared.

Situation	Who owns the problem	Why?	What to do?
Your children are being loud and rowdy at a restaurant.	Parent	The restaurant is a public place. The children's noise is disturbing other patrons and interfering with your enjoyment of the meal.	*Discipline
Your child rides their bike on a busy street.	Parent	This problem involves the child's safety. It is the parents' responsibility to teach and enforce safety rules.	*Discipline
Your daughter doesn't like her sister going into her room without asking.	Child	Siblings are entitled to have a relationship with each other without parents interfering. The sisters need to learn how to work together and get along.	Support for both children
Your child complains that his teacher picks on him.	Child (unless the teacher is clearly abusive)	Children have relationships with other adults. They need to learn how to relate to them on their own	Support (If abuse or other serious problems exist, the parent needs to intervene.)
Your child has a temper tantrum in the supermarket.	Parent	The child's behavior is interfering with the parent's goal of shopping, as well as that of other shoppers.	*Discipline

Your six-year-old complains that they are being picked on by ten-year-olds.	Shared	This would be the child's problem, except that the age difference makes it beyond his level of maturity to handle.	Support for the child and intervention with the other children's parents.
Your child is not keeping up with their schoolwork.	Shared	The parent's goal of the child being successful in school is blocked, yet school success is also the responsibility of the child.	Support and *discipline

Chart used with the permission of the publisher. [84]

*The word *Discipline* means *to teach*. More in Chapter Twelve

How Can We Help Heal and Bless Our Children?

Jesus looked at the individual's needs to figure out what role He could play in their healing. We can do this as well. Looking at who owns the problem helps us heal and bless our children. When we stop and think about who owns the problem, it helps us to know what role to play. Knowing that Jesus also thought about the role He could play in helping someone to heal and grow can guide our actions with our loved ones. Letting this be one of the first things we do helps us avoid issues.

Doing too much or too little for our children can have consequences that it would be better to avoid. Kids don't like it when we are too controlling and do things they can do for themselves. The opposite is also true: if we are not involved enough, they can get in over their heads and struggle because their burden is too heavy. Figuring out who owns problems early on helps parents avoid power struggles and rebellion. It also helps us avoid unnecessary pain by doing too little. Let's walk through the roles we can play in problem-solving.

If you determine the child owns the problem, then your role is to support the child as they solve the problem. Encourage them to explain the problem and just listen. If their thinking is off, letting them explain it to you may help them fix their thinking. Look for the feelings they are struggling through and offer encouragement. Encourage them to come up with ways to solve their current problem. Compliment them on their ideas and,

---

84   Michael H. Popkin, *Active Parenting: A Parent's Guide to Raising Happy and Successful Children*. (Marietta: Active Parenting Publishers. 2014) 49.

if necessary, remind them of past successes with solving problems. In the workbook portion of this chapter, I have included a decision-making chart that can help a child work through a problem and look at the possible outcomes safely with you.

If the problem is owned by the child, let them solve it as much on their own as they can. You'll know they own the problem if they are the ones that are directly affected by the problem, or if they were the ones that brought the problem to your attention. Check in with them about it, but don't try and solve it for them. If your son doesn't like his brother "borrowing" his Legos. He can talk to his brother on his own. They can solve a problem they are having with each other without us getting in the middle of it. (They may need help discovering that they are capable of handling this one on their own, but that is easily done with a quick conversation. You can even let them practice on you.)

Shared Ownership of the Problem

If the problem is shared, your role may be to give them some behind-the-scenes support to work with them to solve the problem. You may determine that the child needs more support because of the child's age, or if the severity of the problem warrants more involvement from you.

I was working with a group of girls for Primary activities and teaching them to use the decision making chart to solve problems. A girl named Rebecca had been dealing with a bully who forced her to share her answers during a test. It was eating her up inside, and she didn't want it to happen again. By filling out this chart, she worked out a solution. It was wonderful to see her role-play this solution with some of her Primary friends. She and I talked to her mom when she picked Rebecca up. I could see her countenance was lighter as she left the Primary room.

The next time I saw Rebecca, she wore the biggest smile and gave me a big hug. When I asked her what the hug was for, she said she had faced her giant and defeated it. I was so happy for her. When Rebecca wrote out her worry, she found a solution. Her parents' support helped her feel confident about handling the situation. If the bully was threatening Rebecca with bodily harm, then her parents should step in. Through questioning and inspiration, we can often help others sift through issues that arise. We can work together to come up with plans to solve problems where each person has a part in the solution.

What About Parent-Owned Problems?

How we can help our children heal if we own the problem? Sometimes our children need us to take on the burden because it is too much for them. Similarly, we saw Jesus heal Mary Magdalene. She couldn't heal herself. She needed the healing touch of Jesus Christ. Children sometimes need us to remove burdens when the burden is too heavy for them, or because the burden is not something that concerns them.

The child's age and maturity level will help us determine what they can take on. Jesus understood what Mary could do and acted accordingly. If the problem involves health, safety, or family rules/values, the parent owns the problem. Taking the time to listen will help you determine ownership. Prayer also helps us to know what role to play and when we need to step in.

Determining whether we own the problem is the first step. Parent-owned problems give us a chance to establish boundaries, communicate our expectations, and, at times, discipline or teach our children. (We'll talk about the ins and outs of discipline in chapters ten and eleven. The art of teaching and directing our children has a lot of facets, and for now, let's concentrate on recognizing and owning problems.)

We may be tempted to pass a problem on to someone else, but if we take ownership of the problem it is up to us to solve it. Take it on and be an example of one who is not afraid to work through a problem. Avoid pushing it off onto someone else. If you are at a park and your child is getting bullied by older children, make your presence known and let your child know you have their back. Or if a ball goes over your fence and you have not met your neighbors, it may be time to meet them, even though you were comfortable on your couch. Try to be aware of the challenges your children are facing and help when needed.

If we are the ones to bring up a problem, it is usually ours to own. We may need to set boundaries to keep children safe and us sane. Setting boundaries eases burdens because children understand expectations. Parents are in charge of making sure the boundaries meet the needs of the children and help them feel safe. They also help us feel safe and comfortable instead of feeling anxious. Let's tackle setting and maintaining boundaries first.

For example, if a child has broken the family rule about climbing on the kitchen cupboards to get a treat off the fridge, the parent owns this problem. There is a family rule involved, and the safety of a child is at play. Both these things are categories the parents own. The following conversation could take place.

"Chase, it looks like you found the cookies I was saving for after dinner. How did you get one?"

Chase may not say much because he is trying to figure out how you knew about the cookies. (Could it be the chocolate on his face?) Since he is tongued-tied, you might ask, "Why might I be concerned about this?"

Chase may say something like, "But mom, I was SO hungry, and they smelled SO good!"

We might say, "Why do you think I'd be concerned about you getting the cookies off the top of the fridge?"

Chase may use distraction tactics at this stage by saying, "But Mom, I am a growing boy and I need to eat."

We may say, "I know you are getting big, but that does not change the family rule. What is our family rule about climbing?"

Chase may choose to say the family rule in an exasperated tone of voice, "Don't climb on the cupboards because you may break something or yourself."

If your questions finally lead the discussion to your expectations you can say, "I am glad you know the family rule. Since you broke this one, you will not get a cookie after dinner. You already ate yours. I hope you will make better choices next time."

Another reason a parent owns a problem is when we are the ones concerned about it. Kids rarely worry about embarrassing us by fighting in public or making a lot of noise in a restaurant, but these can be big deals to us. This makes the problem ours because we are the ones bothered by what is happening or not happening with our children. Do our children have a clear view of what we expect of them in a public place? Have we taken the time to explain expectations? Setting expectations helps everyone to feel safe and secure.

Here is another example that illustrates this point. Think about the last time you took your kids to a band concert or a play, and your children were noisy and disruptive. To avoid a repeat of this, before going to a concert, the following discussion could take place.

"I would like to talk to you about my expectations during the band concert. Last time we did well sitting quietly until the fourth song, and then we got restless and noisy. I think we can make it through the whole concert this time. I am afraid our behavior made it hard for others around us to hear the music. What could we do to be more respectful of the others and the kids performing?"

Take ideas and then practice the concert behavior. Follow up the discussion by thanking them and then establishing consequences if they do not meet expectations. "I love your ideas and am excited to go to the concert with you. I know it can be long, but we have a plan now. If you forget to be quiet, I will give you one warning. If you are still noisy, you'll need to come sit by me. Does everyone understand?"

If expectations are met, follow through with your plan. If they are not met, simply say, "I'm sorry you chose to be noisy. Come sit by me." (This can be said without words by pointing to the chair and motioning for them to come sit by you.) This simple follow-through helps children make the connection between their behavior and the positive and negative consequences.

Noticing Needs Communicates Love and Promotes Healing

The Savior went about easing the burdens of others, and we can do this as well. We can communicate our love to others by noticing when they need help. Then, by determining who owns the problem, we can determine which role to play. This helps everyone feel more safe and secure. It is up to us to be the Savior's hands with our loved ones. Learning to recognize our role can ease burdens and help hearts and homes to stay well and whole.

Jesus stepped in and healed people that needed his tender care. Mary Magdalene couldn't cast the demons out by herself. The man who was born blind could do the washing, but he couldn't heal his eyes. The woman with the issue of blood could reach out and touch Jesus, but she couldn't do the actual healing herself. His willingness to enter people's stories, ease burdens, and heal hearts is a beautiful thing. He let people do as much for themselves as they could. We can follow His example with our children.

How Do We Transfer Ownership of a Problem from Us to a Child/Teen/Young Adult?

As parents, we can sometimes carry the burdens of others needlessly. Kids grow up too fast, and that means their abilities are also changing rapidly. One day children can't tie their shoes and the next day they are completely capable of doing this. But we sometimes don't notice their changing abilities. (Why am I still washing your clothes and you're twenty?)

If you discover that you need to pass the ownership of a problem or responsibility to someone else, here are some pointers:

- Define and own the problem: Simply state the problem that needs to be addressed and recognize that you are the one who has been handling the problem.

- Pass ownership to the child: "I realized that you are capable of tying your own shoes. I'm sorry that I kept tying them even though you knew how. From now on, I'm going to expect you to tie your own shoes."

- Remind them of ability: Share memories of past times when they did the task, or other similar tasks, to help them see they are capable. It also sends them the message you believe in them.

- Use birthdays to pass responsibility on to a child: "Now that you are six, you can tie your own shoes just like you make your bed."

- Ask yourself the following question: "Am I doing things for my kids they can do for themselves?" Resist the urge to do something for them just because it's easier, less messy, and/or takes less time.

- Give them the tools they need to solve the problem: Teach them the skills necessary to be successful, and be patient with them as they learn.

- Remember to never do anything for a child that they can do for themselves: We are trying to work ourselves out of a job!

The following is my favorite example of transferring ownership from the Active Parenting classes I took and taught. It is from a video vignette that shows a mother successfully transferring ownership of a problem to her daughter. She owned her daughter's morning problem and didn't want it anymore. The following is how she transferred the ownership of this problem to her daughter.

"Emily, you are going to be late for school again if you don't wake up!" I yelled from the kitchen.

My daughter's response was one I had heard countless times, "Why didn't you wake me up sooner!? Now I am going to be late for school and it is all your fault!"

Was it my fault? I wondered. I realized that somehow her morning problem had become my problem. She was fifteen and would soon be off to college, and I wondered who would wake her up there. I realized this was one problem that didn't need to be mine. I decided I would talk to her and give the problem back to her. She made it to school, but she was late. That night, I decided we would have a little chat. We were both calm, and I started our conversation like this. "I've noticed that you are having a hard time waking up in the morning for school. Why is that?"

"If you would just wake me up on time, I could make it to school. It's your fault!" she said as she angrily folded her arms.

I stayed calm and said, "I'm sorry it has become a problem for you."

She then said, "Yeah, I've been late to Spanish so many times it is affecting my grade."

"I'm sorry to hear that. How about we find a solution instead of dealing with the same problem day after day and expecting different results?" We then brainstormed about why she was having this problem and things we could do about it. She agreed to get to bed by 10 p.m. and I agreed she could use the car if she left the house by 7:40. If she didn't leave by then, she would have to ride the bus the next day.

I also turned the chore of waking herself up back over to her by saying, "I realized this morning that you are fifteen years old. You are old enough to get yourself up in the morning. You do so many other hard things and you can do this as well. You'll have to do this at college, unless you want me to come with you. So, from now on, I won't be waking you up." She liked the fact that I noticed the things she was doing and that she was growing up. We even laughed at the thought of me going with her to college. We made sure her alarm clock worked, and we also set her alarm on her phone. The next day she came down ready to go, and I let her know how much I appreciated her taking ownership of this problem. She really could tackle her morning problem. She just needed to own it, and have support to work through the problem.[85]

By passing ownership of the problem to her daughter, this mother sent the message that she saw her daughter as capable and confident of handling *her* morning problem. This acknowledgment can be very freeing and healing to everyone involved.

Some of the issues we see around us are a lack of people being willing to take on their own problems and trying to push them onto someone else. Many problems would go away if we owned them. We are capable and able to take on hard things and we can help our children learn to do this as well. The workbook will give you a chance to recognize and practice this important skill.

---

85   Michael H. Popkin, *Active Parenting: A Parent's Guide to Raising Happy and Successful Children*, 4th Edition, videos, (Marietta, Active Parenting Publishers, 2014) videos. Used with Permission.

Intentional Healing

Workbook

What Role Do I Play?

Part of helping people to heal or overcome problems is to understand the role we play in helping our family members grow and learn. Work through the following situations to determine who owns the problem.

1. Your six-year-old is in charge of setting the table. He is capable of setting the table. He is just distracted. Should you set the table? Why or why not?

_____

_____

_____

_____

2. Your fifteen-year-old injured his hand, but needs to start using it more. You are playing cards together. Do you take over the job of shuffling the cards? Why or why not?

_____

_____

_____

_____

3. Your fifteen-year-old relies on you to pack his lunch and do his laundry. You feel that he needs to be in charge of this. How can you shift ownership of this problem to your teen?

_____

_____

_____

_____

4. Look at the problems that have lately arisen in your family. Pick a problem to work through. Determine who owns the problem so that you know which role to play. Use the chart in this chapter to help you with this. Ask yourself whether you share the responsibility, own it, or the child owns it. How can you offer support that will promote the most growth?

_____

_____

_____

_____

How to Avoid Issues

1. Choose an issue in which your child's behavior might conflict with your expectations and cause a problem. (For example: being left home alone, having friends over for the evening, using the car, or going on a date.)

Follow these steps to help avoid potential problems. Write down what you might do and say before you talk to your child about the problem you are having.

Step 1: Define the problem. Think about all the questions you have about the potential problem and try to anticipate problems that may occur. This way you can ask your child how they will handle various scenarios so that you can both avoid problems and praise them for how they would handle things that come up.

Step 2: Let everyone share thoughts and feelings. This gives both of you a chance to express the things that are important to you or things you are worried about.

Step 3: Brainstorm solutions. By working together and talking through possible issues, you can come up with solutions. During this phase, try not to be critical of anyone's ideas. Just jot them down without judgment.

Step 4: Come up with a plan that both can agree upon. Ask the child what they think would be a fair consequence if they don't meet expectations. Look at the ideas you generated and star or circle the ones that seem to be the best solution for the problem at hand.

Step 5: Decide on logical consequences if guidelines are not followed. If consequences are agreed upon before things occur, then the child understands expectations instead of just guessing what is expected. (We'll learn more about this in the next chapter.)

Step 6: Try it out. Give them a chance to prove that they can do something. Show confidence in their ability and let them do things within the parameters you have set together. If they make a mistake, let the consequences teach. Offer love and let them try again after you troubleshoot what went wrong.

Step 7: Follow up after the event in question to give children/teens feedback on how they did.[86]

What did you like about how your talk went?

_____

_____

_____

_____

---

86   Michael H. Popkin, *Active Parenting: a Parent's Guide to Raising Happy and Successful Children,* (Marietta: Active Parenting Publishers, 2014), 102-103.

What will you do differently next time?

_____

_____

_____

_____

Do you think your talk helped prevent any problems this week? If so, which ones?

_____

_____

_____

_____

If problems occurred, did you follow through with logical consequences (See Chapter Twelve)? If so, how did it go?

_____

_____

_____

_____

Decision-Making Chart

This decision-making chart is one I have used with my kids, for Primary activities, my students at school, and myself. Taking the time to think through hard choices allows us to be courageous and do hard things. It also helps us to predict the consequences of our actions. Use the scenarios in this chart or come up with your own that apply to your kids. This empowers kids to make good choices. Spending time working through problems shows our children we care about the choices they make.

Decision-Making Chart

Sometimes when you have a choice to make it helps to write out your options and think about what the consequences might be. In the space below, work through a decision you need to make.

Dilemma

Brainstorm some possible ways to handle this situation and put your choices in the boxes below.

Choice #1	Choice #2	Choice #3
Pros:	Pros:	Pros:
Cons:	Cons:	Cons:

Which choice will you choose? Which of these choices best reflects who I am trying to become?

_____

_____

_____

_____

Decision Making Training

The goal of these activities is to provide children and parents with a clear outline and opportunity to practice making decisions. Children can:

- Recognize and understand the steps to make good decisions.
- Learn to stop and think about their choices before they act.
- Analyze the consequences of the choices they might make.
- Role-play these scenarios and practice making choices.
- Gain more autonomy as they demonstrate good character.

The following are scenarios both serious and fun that can be used to help children learn to be better decision makers. Print off the situations and have your kids pick a situation out of a hat to role-play.

I created these to help my students think about the choices they were making that affected who they were becoming. Children today are bombarded with decisions. We want our children to understand they are responsible for the choices they make. These scenarios are for grade-school-aged children. You can adapt them to the birds in your nest. Have fun with this, and empower your children to be good decision-makers.

Academic Integrity

1. During a test, you realize that you can see your neighbor's answers and you didn't study for this test. What will you do?
2. Your sister offered to trade you jobs. She would do your math homework if you do the dishes. What will you do?
3. You have a sub and some of the kids are answering to the wrong name. What will you do?
4. For the intervention hour, you are not in the group you think you should be in. What will you do?
5. You are bored in class. What will you do?

Respect

6. The two kids you are sitting next to at lunch start making fun of the new kid in class. What will you do?
7. You thought you handed in a math paper, but your teacher can't find it. What will you do?
8. At recess, a friend of yours is being bullied. You are worried about him/her. What will you do?

Honesty

9. The student next to you brought five dollars to school. It fell out of his desk. What will you do?

Empathy

> 10. One of the kids in your class just dropped a whole stack of papers he was trying to pass out. What will you do?
> 11. Your friend has to have surgery on her foot and will miss school. You want to help. What will you do?

Responsibility

> 12. You are supposed to have your parents sign a permission slip to go on a field trip, and one to say that they have seen your report card, but you don't want them to see your report card. What will you do?
> 13. The kitchen is a disaster. You don't feel like you made the mess, but you don't get to play a game until the mess is cleaned up. What will you do?

Knight Training

Here are some fun situations you could use to introduce decision-making to your kids. These scenarios are a bit out there. I used them in a school setting when we were doing "Knight Training." I found that if I got their attention at the beginning of a learning activity, I could get them engaged in the learning. After they were engaged, I could move to more serious problems to solve. These situations could be used to train your children to "put on the whole armor of God."

Courage

> 1. One day, you and your little sister were walking through the forest when a giant troll comes out of the forest. How would you handle this situation? What would you do?

Dependability

> 2. The Lady of the Manor assigned you to protect her children. You would rather be defending the castle. How will you treat the children you are guarding?

Compassion

> 3. A fellow knight has no food to eat. What would you do?

Patience

> 4. A fellow knight cannot juggle. You are good at it. He asks you to teach him how to juggle. Teaching someone to juggle can be hard and time-consuming. What would you do?

Perseverance

5. You are to deliver a note to the king from Lord Ludwig. The weather is horrible and you hate being cold? What would you do?

Loyalty

6. Your friend is getting picked on by the biggest knight. You want to help your friend, but he is really big. What would you do?

Tolerance

7. You are asked to work with a knight you don't like because he smells bad. What would you do?

8. A knight wants to be a part of your patrol group. His accent is thick, and he walks with a limb. How will you treat him?

Dealing with Setbacks

9. You are usually really good at archery, but you were not selected to be an archer and are put in a group to practice archery. What is Lord Ludwig thinking?!?! You are not happy about having to practice something you are already good at. How will you act? Will you act sad (mope) and treat others around you badly? Or will you take the chance to get better and have a good attitude? What will be the consequences of each of these ways of dealing with your current dilemma?

10. In the archery group, you learn how it feels to not be selected. Was it hard to not be selected? How will you choose to deal with little setbacks? How will you have a good attitude? What decisions can you make to show that this setback did not defeat you?

Honesty

11. Another knight caught you cheating in an archery contest. You know it is wrong to cheat. How will you do better in the future? You are about to play a game of checkers with him. What can you do to restore his faith in you?

Chapter Ten

Agency and Responsibility

The Power of Choice

Our family waited for ten minutes to go to church one Sunday because Natale, our six-year-old, refused to put on her shoes. (Does this sound familiar?) Those were a long ten minutes full of whining, pleading, and threatening. . . and this was from me! My husband came on the scene, saw the dilemma, and walked away without a lot of explanation. He came back a minute later with a pair of Sunday shoes that didn't match her cute outfit quite as well but would work.

He handed the shoes to me and said, "Let her choose which ones she wants to wear."

I bent down and said, "Which would you like to wear?" Of course, she chose the ones that didn't match. But a minute later, we were all headed out the door.

Now some of you are thinking, "I would have given her a choice to put on the first shoes or spend time in her room." The problem with this choice is that we wouldn't have been any closer to getting out the door. And Natale may have come to resent me because I forced her hand. This type of resentment can grow and cause genuine hurt in a relationship. Giving her a choice gave her some power without her having to say "no" to get it!

Later that day, after I had apologized, I asked her why she didn't want to wear the shoes. She said, "They hurt my feet." I had her go get them and sure enough, they were too small. In the heat of the moment, I missed this major detail. I was too close to the situation and forgot about the power of choice (Parenting 101- choice diffuses power struggles). I was grateful for my husband's suggestion. (Okay, at first, I was annoyed, but I got over it quickly when it solved our problem.)

Natale knew something that I didn't, and she didn't want to be forced to do something that would bring her pain. Respecting our children's needs and right to choose has some inherent risks. The Savior understood the power of choice, and His example can help us to teach our children to be responsible. The power to choose is something that has always been a hot topic.

Agency and Responsibility

From the very beginning of time, Heavenly Father wanted us to have the ability to choose for ourselves. The gift of Agency is a crucial element of Heavenly Father's Plan of Happiness. It was discussed in the Council in Heaven where we determined whether we would be given the ability to choose for ourselves how we would live our lives. Our Heavenly Father presented a plan that gave us a chance to choose for ourselves how we would live. He understood the importance of being responsible for our own actions.[87] Our brother, Jesus Christ, was willing to carry out the plan presented by our Father.

Lucifer also presented a plan that he claimed would ensure that none of Heavenly Father's children would be lost. Satan made it sound good, but it was a lie. He is the father of lies after all. He wanted the power and glory for himself.

Jesus wanted His Father to be the one who received the glory. He never forced people to follow Him. He always allows choice. We see evidence of this throughout the scriptures. Part of the Great Plan of Happiness was for us to come to earth to be tested. Part of that test was giving us the responsibility and opportunity to choose for ourselves what we will do while on this earth, and who we will choose to follow.

Sharon G. Larson reminds us what agency is in the following quote, "Agency is the power to think, choose, and act for ourselves. It comes with endless opportunities, accompanied by responsibility and consequences. It is a blessing and a burden. Using this gift of agency wisely is critical today because never in the world's history have God's children been so blessed or so blatantly confronted with so many choices."[88]

In this section, we will explore how responsibility is directly tied to making choices. We will explore how we can help our children use the gift of agency wisely and look at the positive and negative consequences our choices

87   Moses 4:1-4.

88   Sharon G. Larson, "Agency-A Blessing and a Burden," *Ensign*, November 1999.

create. Helping our children learn to be responsible means we will help them become good decision-makers in a world where choices are endless and consequences don't seem to be attached to these choices. (How many times does Wile E. Coyote get smashed by a boulder only to get back up? Actions seem to have no consequences.)

His Example

Jesus used His agency wisely throughout His life. With every choice, He exercised His agency and a willingness to do His Father's will. Our opportunities will increase when we also choose to do our Heavenly Father's will. In the following quote, Elder Robert D. Hales reminds us how Jesus used His agency wisely and how essential agency is to Heavenly Father's plan.

> Throughout His life, our Savior showed us how to use our agency. As a boy in Jerusalem, He deliberately chose to 'be about [His] Father's business.' In His ministry, He obediently chose 'to do the will of [His] Father.' In Gethsemane, He chose to suffer all things, saying, 'Not my will, but thine, be done. And there appeared an angel unto him from heaven, strengthening him.' On the cross, He chose to love His enemies, praying, 'Father, forgive them; for they know not what they do.' And then, so that He could finally demonstrate that He was choosing for Himself, He was left alone. '[Father,] why hast thou forsaken me?' He asked. At last, He exercised His agency to act, enduring to the end, until He could say, 'It is finished.'
>
> Though He 'was in all points tempted like as we are,' with every choice and every action He exercised the agency to be our Savior—to break the chains of sin and death for us. And by His perfect life, He taught us that when we choose to do the will of our Heavenly Father, our agency is preserved, our opportunities increase, and we progress.[89]

This quote reminds us of the magnitude of the Savior's choices and the example He set for us. His actions preserved our agency. We can progress because of Him, and are freer when we learn to make good choices. Our choices determine who we will become more than our abilities. It is what we do with the gifts we have been given that determine who we are. Christ's decisions set Him apart from others. His example can lead us to be free today and tomorrow and forever.

---

89   Robert D. Hales, "Agency: Essential to the Plan of Life," *Ensign*, November 2010.

Throughout His earthly ministry, Jesus emphasized the worth of the individual and their ability to choose for themselves who they will follow. He never forced anyone to follow Him. He understood the importance and responsibility associated with this freedom to choose. It was something He respected. Jesus's awareness of this is evident in His teachings.

The ancient disciples were given the opportunity to choose to follow Him or continue fishing.[90] The rich young ruler had a choice to follow the Savior or not.[91] Jesus let it be their choice. We are also given this same freedom to choose. We have a similar invitation. Will we "leave our nets behind" and follow Him? We are the ones responsible for the nets we cast. It can be tricky, but with the Savior as our guide, we can use this precious gift wisely, and help our children learn to use it wisely as well.

Elder Renlund helps us understand the importance of choice. His explanation sheds light on what we can strive for in our families. Obedience needs to be a choice. He said,

> Our Heavenly Father's goal in parenting is not to have His children *do* what is right; it is to have His children *choose* to do what is right and ultimately become like Him. If He simply wanted us to be obedient, He would use immediate rewards and punishments to influence our behaviors.
>
> But God is not interested in His children just becoming trained and obedient 'pets' who will not chew on His slippers in the celestial living room. No, God wants His children to grow up spiritually and join Him in the family business.[92]

Elder Renlund helps us to understand that we need to be more than a "trained pet" who does what he is asked to do. Heavenly Father wants us to become like Him and His Son. To be able to do this, we need to go beyond compliance to being willing to do things because we love God and His ways, and not just to avoid punishment.

Agency is a precious gift and important in parenting. We are free to choose, but that does not mean this freedom is without cost. Agency is not free. Christ paid this debt for us. Satan does everything he can to rob us of this gift. He wants us to be slaves to our passions and vices, and he wants us to be miserable like him.

The responsibility of making choices falls on each of us. It is one of the greatest gifts we've been given from our Heavenly Father. We are given the

90   Matthew 4:18-22.
91   Matthew 19:16-22; Mark 10:17-22.
92   Dale G. Renlund, "Choose Ye This Day," *Ensign*, November 2018.

opportunity to choose for ourselves which path we will take. This ability to choose has some inherent risks. The biggest is that we might not make the right choice. Parents struggle with this as well. We don't want to see our kids get hurt or have negative consequences. We want to give our children a chance to make their own decisions, but what if they make a mistake? This is why we have the Savior and His infinite Atonement, and this is all part of the Great Plan of Happiness.

Responsible, Intentional Parenting

We are bombarded with choices every day. We make so many decisions in a single day that it boggles the mind. Helping our children be good decision-makers is one of the biggest responsibilities we have. That is why it is so important that our homes are safe places for everyone to make choices and learn from the consequences. We want our children to learn that they are responsible for the choices they make. They can choose for themselves, but they can't choose the consequences that will follow their choice.

One way of looking at responsibility is to turn it into an equation:

$$\text{Choice} + \text{Consequences} = \text{Responsibility}.[93]$$

This helps us remember that helping our children to be responsible means we help them understand the relationship between their choices and the consequences of their actions.

Watching how Jesus Christ uses His agency helps us to know how to use our own agency. He chooses to follow His Father with every decision He makes. We can do likewise. We can do our best to follow Him. We can do our best to give our children meaningful ways to use their agency.

It starts when they are little, giving them small things to choose between, like: "Do you want to wear these shoes or these?" or "Do you want milk or orange juice?" As they age, we can give them more and more choices within the boundaries we set. We make fewer and fewer decisions for them, and our boundaries are less restricting and ever-expanding until they set their own boundaries and limits.

In a world that seems to have no boundaries and an endless amount of choices, helping our children use their agency wisely is one of our toughest jobs! This challenge does not need to overwhelm us. Our Heavenly Father loves us and wants us to be happy. He has given us commandments not to limit our fun, but to help us be safe and find happiness in this ever changing

---

93   Popkin, 2014

world. We are given examples in the scriptures to help us teach our children about the choices they are making. The scriptures can help us in this as well.

If, Then Statements

Throughout the scriptures, there are many "if, then" statements. These statements let us know what our Heavenly Father expects us to do and what He will do in return. There are almost 900 of these statements in the Old Testament alone. The Book of Mormon has almost 600 "if, then" statements.[94] We can learn so much from this type of expectation.

We can learn so much from this type of expectation. An example of an "if, then" statement is found in 2 Nephi 1:20: "And he hath said that: Inasmuch as he shall keep my commandments ye shall prosper in the land; but inasmuch as you will not keep my commandments ye shall be cut off from my presence."

Here are a few more "if, then" statements to look up: 1 Nephi 17:50; 2 Nephi 1:20; Mosiah 16:6-7; Alma 48:15-16; 2 Chronicles 7:14, and Isaiah 1:19. These patterns are throughout the scriptures.

God wants to bless us and help us here on this earth. Blessings follow obedience, but that doesn't mean they are immediate. The blessings are tied to our willingness to follow Him. We change when we are willing to follow Him. God does not punish people. People punish themselves by how they choose to behave. What we see as "punishment" is often the self-imposed, natural consequences of the choices we make.

Our children can learn similarly. We can follow the pattern we see throughout the scriptures. We can tie things together either logically or naturally to help motivate our children to make good choices. "If, then" statements allow the consequences to do the teaching for us, and allow us to show compassion when negative consequences follow actions. We are also able to rejoice with our children when they do what is asked, and watch the sense of accomplishment they feel when they have a good consequence. The following story is from a mom I took some parenting classes with. Her son Bryce experienced the consequences of his actions and learned a great deal.

---

94 Norton Oak, "Principles of the Gospel of Jesus Christ and If/Then Logic," *Scripture Notes*, https://scripturenotes.com/principles-of-the-gospel-of-jesus-christ-and-if-then-logic Accessed Oct. 31, 2023.

I'm Only Going to Wash What Is in the Hamper

My son Bryce's room was a disaster. He was eleven and his dirty clothes were strewn all over his room. I thought I was clever for putting a hamper that looked like a basketball hoop in his room. Either he was a terrible shot, or he had forgotten about the existence of the hamper. I was sick of the mess and the smell. During family council, I let all the kids know I would only wash the clothes in their hampers. They wouldn't be washed if they didn't make it in their hamper.

Two weeks later, Bryce came to breakfast in his pajamas on a school day. The rule at our house was that they could eat breakfast after they were dressed. I asked him if it was a pajama day. He said it wasn't, and that he didn't have any clean clothes. I told him I was sorry to hear that. I reminded him I had washed all the clothes in the hamper three days ago. The light dawned on him. His hamper had dust on it.

He then said, "I can't wear pajamas to school. What am I going to wear?" I could muster some concern for his predicament and sent him back to his room. When he came out of his room in his church clothes, minus the tie, I was a bit surprised but hid it. He went to school that way, and his dirty clothes seemed to make it in the hamper after that. I've often wondered what others said to him that day. It was great that he learned a lesson without me saying anything to him.

- Kerry Eaton, La Luz, New Mexico, USA

This was such a fun story to hear Kerry tell. Who doesn't have a child with this type of problem? I love how Kerry let the natural consequences do the teaching. She could be a concerned listener and express sympathy for his predicament, but allow the consequence to follow. This type of teaching is impactful and encourages change!

Natural Consequences

Now let's look at natural consequences. Our children are quick learners, and learn through direct experiences. Natural consequences are great teachers. When we make our homes safe places to learn, lives change. It takes courage not to intervene on our children's behalf. It takes courage to let them make mistakes and learn from those mistakes.

Natural consequences are the natural repercussions of a child's behavior. Natural consequences are very effective in teaching independence. When the consequences happen, parents have an opportunity to show empathy to the child for the consequences. (Just like my friend Kerry did.)

It takes courage to not intervene on our children's behalf. It takes courage to let them make mistakes and learn from them. Elder Richard G. Scott of the Quorum of the Twelve Apostles said, "Parents, don't make the mistake of purposefully intervening to soften or eliminate the natural consequences of your child's deliberate decisions to violate the commandments. Such acts reinforce false principles, open the door for more serious sin, and lessen the likelihood of repentance."[95]

Courageous parents allow their children to make mistakes without rescuing them from the consequences. It takes courage to be okay with children making their own decisions. We can give them the support and boundaries they need to be successful and safe, both spiritually and physically. Agency is a powerful gift and letting our children exercise their agency takes courage. Here are some examples of Natural Consequences:

- The natural consequence of leaving your rollerblades outside is that they can get ruined. They can get rusty, lost, or "borrowed." If this happens, parents can offer sympathy for the loss of the rollerblades. The timing of this consequence may be too far away for a child to make the connection. Parents could say something like, "Are those your rollerblades? What might happen to them if you leave them outside for a week or longer?" Let them answer and then they can choose what they'll do.

- The natural consequence of eating too much is getting a bellyache. The question for parents to gently ask is something like, "I'm sorry you are not feeling well. Why do you think you have a bellyache? What can you do differently to avoid a bellyache in the future?"

- The natural consequence of staying up too late is that you are tired the next day. Here is an example of a possible way to let the natural consequences teach. "How are you doing today? If they say they are tired, the follow-up question might be, "Why do you think that is?" Kids want to blame their tiredness on how early they have to wake up, but they would be better off if they made the connection with how late they went to bed.

We can set boundaries to help our children be successful. These boundaries keep the child and others safe. We are not going to let a child run into a busy street to experience the natural consequences of their choice. Think

---

95   Richard G. Scott, "The Power of Correct Principles," *Ensign*, May 1993.

freedom within limits. When children are small, the boundaries are close. They can expand as the child ages and show they can handle more responsibility. We eventually work ourselves out of job, but that is a good thing. We want our kids to take on more and more responsibility until they make all of their own decisions.

"If, then" statements are valuable tools that we can use to teach our children how to use their agency, just like Heavenly Father and Jesus use them to help us understand how our choices lead to blessings. Our children's choices have consequences, and we can let these consequences teach our children valuable lessons.

Logical Consequences

Logical consequences occur when parents link a negative or positive consequence to a child's choice. For example, if Jake breaks the family rule and is on his phone after nine o'clock, he loses the privilege of using his phone for two days. This is a logical consequence because it is connected to the misbehavior and was meant to be a consequence of a choice (Remember: Choice + Consequence = Responsibility). If Jake was reminded of the consequence in a firm, but friendly way, it is a consequence and will help him learn to be responsible.

It can become a punishment if the consequence is not logically tied to the choice. For instance, if Jake uses his phone after nine o'clock, and then his mom angrily grounds him from using the car for a month. This becomes a punishment because it is meant to teach obedience and not responsibility. It is also more of a retaliation for a misbehavior than a logical consequence. It has the potential to cause Jake to resent his mom. Resentment is not the goal. Responsibility is what we are after.[96]

Parents sometimes employ spanking as a punishment for misbehavior. Proverbs 13:24 is often used to justify spanking. Some refer to this as the "spare the rod, spoil the child" verse. It says, "He that spareth his rod, hateth his son: but he that loveth him chasteneth him betimes." So what is this rod mentioned here, and how will our children become spoiled if we do not correct them at times with it?

There are several definitions of the word rod that are worth exploring that may help us understand what is meant by this scripture. A rod does not only mean a thin, straight bar made of wood or metal. My former Bishop, Dr. Glenn Latham explores some other meanings of this word, he says: "The

---

96   Michael H. Popkin, *Active Parenting: A Parent's Guide to Raising Happy and Successful Children*, 4th Edition, (Marietta, Active Parenting Publishers, 2014), 91.

word rod has multiple meanings in and out of scripture, to a biblical shepherd, the rod was used to protect the sheep from the wolves. It was used for guiding the sheep. In Psalms, the rod is cited as the source of comfort: "Thy rod and thy staff they comfort me" (Ps. 23:4). It was used to separate the sheep from the goats. With its crook on the end, it was used to recover lambs from danger. In the book of Exodus (4:1-5), the "rod" is the authority of God, interpreted by some to also mean the word of God."[97]

Dr. Latham and I discussed this scripture, and he said it made more sense that a child could be spoiled if the "Word of God" had not been shared with them. In Dr. Latham's Christlike Parenting book, he also said, "It is distressing that of the many positive uses and meanings of the "rod," humankind has chosen to focus on the one punitive use: to beat up on kids. It is another sad example of how, over the ages, humankind has distorted good to justify evil. Once people become convinced that God is on their side, and that what they are doing is done in the name of God, anything is possible—including unspeakable carnage, savagery, horrors, and mayhem."[98]

Spanking is a punishment and something to be avoided. We can look for natural or logical consequences to tie to the choices our children make. We can find better ways to help our children become more responsible without resorting to spanking. Spanking often leads to more misbehaviors. You may get immediate results, but it often leads to retaliation. According to Dr. Latham, "Rather than correcting "bad" behavior, spanking teaches a child that when someone does something annoying or frustrating or causes one to be angry, the way to handle that is to strike out physically, to hurt someone. This is a terrible message to deliver to a child."[99]

Reading scriptures brings light to our minds and helps us discover truths. Scriptures give us direction and when parents share them with their children course corrections that last can be made. Scriptures remind us of many things including God's love when we think of His love we are more likely to follow Him. Like the shepherd who uses his rod to keep his lambs safe, we can use the scriptures to guide and protect our lambs and help them find and stay on a path that will keep them safe. The rod can give comfort to the shepherd because he knows he has a way to protect his sheep. Scriptures help us protect our children from the wolves around them.

President Hinckley reminds us of a better way when he said this about his father: "In terms of physical abuse, I have never accepted the principle of "spare the rod and spoil the child." I will be forever grateful for a father who

---

97   Glenn I. Latham, *Christlike Parenting*, (Seattle: Gold Leaf Press, 2002, 49.

98   Glenn I. Latham, *Christlike Parenting*, (Seattle: Gold Leaf Press, 2002), 49.

99   Latham, Glenn I., *The Power of Positive Parenting*, (Logan: P&T Ink, 1993), 171.

never laid a hand in anger upon his children. Somehow, he had the wonderful talent to let them know what was expected of them and to give them encouragement in achieving it.

I am persuaded that violent fathers produce violent sons. I am satisfied that such punishment, in most instances, does more damage than good. Children don't need beating. They need love and encouragement. They need fathers to whom they can look with respect rather than fear. Above all, they need example."[100]

President Hinckley's father's approach to parenting gives us a glimpse of what is possible. We can avoid spanking and help our children to feel God's love by reading His words to them. Teaching children to behave well is more appropriate than hurting a child for behaving badly.[101] Mistakes are opportunities to teach rather than an excuse to punish. Spanking is neither Christlike nor loving and can be avoided. Heavenly Father will bless our efforts to find better ways when we intentionally try to follow His Son, Jesus Christ.

Perspective

When I was nine years old, my dad and I were driving in the mountains above our home in Spring City, Utah. We stopped at a beautiful spot that overlooked the Sanpete Valley. It was thrilling to be up so high. The day was fairly clear, and we could see the entire valley below.

My dad and I studied the valley. We located familiar landmarks. We could see our town and other nearby towns. As we looked closer, we figured out where our home was, where my grandparents' homes were, and where our church was. As we ate lunch, we watched an afternoon thunderstorm roll in. We could see when it was directly over our house. As it went over our town, I wondered how much it rained and what it smelled like. My dad wondered if we had closed the windows at home. Seeing the storm from up above was a breathtaking experience.

As the storm moved on, I will never forget what my dad said. "God knows when we have storms in our lives. He sees the whole picture. God sees the storms come, and He sees them go." God watches over us all, just as my dad and I were watching all that was going on below us. I knew God had a plan for us and that He loves us and, in particular, that He loved me. Having the perspective of the storm from above helped me to understand a little about how God works.

---

100   President Gordon B. Hinckley, "Save the Children," *Ensign*, November 94.
101   Latham, *Christlike Parenting*, 49.

I know we lived in Heaven before we came to Earth. Our existence did not begin at birth, and it won't end at death. He sent us to earth with a plan to get back to Him. His plan was to send us to earth to gain a body, to learn and grow, and to use our gift of agency. He sent His Son, Jesus Christ, to show us the way. He grouped us in families, and He gave us scriptures and prophets to guide us here on Earth.

When storms or trials come our way, we have a choice in how we will face them. Agency is a crucial part of Heavenly Father's plan. We can choose how we will handle the storm, but we can't choose the consequences. My earthly father gave me a glimpse of how Heavenly Father watches over all of us. God knows us and our needs and loves us. He gave us a plan to follow, and I am grateful for my ability to choose. It truly is a gift. Helping my children to learn to use this precious gift has been a challenge and a blessing. Using logical and natural consequences helps us to teach our children about responsibility.

Intentional Responsible Parenting
Workbook

Practice Using the Power of Choice

Before we roll up our sleeves and get to work, let's look at the power of choice for just a minute more. Think about the power of choice. If a child is forced to do something, their only option to gain power is to refuse, like Natale did in our first example. The key is learning what choices to give children. It was better to give Natale a choice between the two pairs of shoes than whether to spend time in her room or wear the shoes. Learning to give good choices takes a bit of practice. We'll do this below.

By giving children "if/then," "when/then," or "either/or" choices, we can eliminate power struggles. Here are a few examples of choices we can give young children: "*If* you practice the piano a half hour a day this week, *then* we can get some more sheet music." "*When* you clean off the table, *then* we can play a game." "Would you rather swing *or* play on the jungle gym?" "Would you like to clear the table *or* sweep the floor tonight?" This not only helps eliminate power struggles, but it also helps children feel confident about making their own decisions. Our children can see that we have confidence in them to complete the task.

For older children, open-ended questions are better. For example, "What kind of drink would you like with your breakfast?" or "How would you like to help with cleaning up tonight?" If a teen says something smart like, "I don't want to help clean tonight," our calm comeback can be, "Choose one of the kitchen jobs, or you can wash the pans. You decide." (Cleaning the pans just happens to be his least favorite job.)

We are not dictators ordering our children around. We can give our children choices. This can decrease the number of tantrums and power struggles. Everything does not need to be a choice, but learning to give choices instead of ordering others around helps us win the cooperation of our family members.

Getting used to giving choices instead of commands takes a bit of work. This week, notice the commands you give your children. Could you give them a choice instead? Write out some things you usually command your children to do in the space below. Change them into a choice. Remember, only give choices you can live with. For instance, "Either pick up your dirty shoes after school or I will throw them in the trash!" This punishes you and your child, and is not logical. Instead, you could say, "If you didn't put your shoes away, you will find them in the junk bin in the basement." This inconveniences the child and encourages them to connect it to their shoes not being put away. Children need clear directions from their parents.

Practice Changing Old Commands into New Choices

Example: Old command: "Put on the clothes I set out for you and hurry!"

New Choice: "I've set out two sets of clothes. You can choose which ones to wear, but breakfast is in five minutes, and I know how hungry you get in the morning. Choose quickly so you won't miss breakfast."

1. What are some of the old commands you would give your children?

_____

_____

_____

_____

2. How did your child respond to the old command?

_____

_____

_____

_____

3. What new choices can you give your children?

_____

_____

_____

_____

4. What was the difference?

_____

_____

_____

_____

5. How did your child respond?

_____

_____

_____

_____

"If, Then" Statements and "When, Then" Statements

How many of us have watched our children "dig in their heels" when we've asked them to brush their teeth or take out the trash? This type of power struggle can be avoided. We can use one of the oldest parenting tools from the Bible: Pairing something you want the child to do with something your child enjoys doing. When the child does the desired thing, then he/she can do the second thing.

Here's an example, "When you have brushed your teeth, then I can read you a story." Read the story after the child brushes his teeth. If the child does not brush his teeth, they go to bed without a story. Be direct and calm, and let the consequence do the teaching for you, even if they cry and carry on about it not being fair. It only has to happen once for them to not want it to happen again. This is not a reward or bribe, but just an application of a "work before play" attitude.

Let's try this!

1. Write down something you would like your child to do, but they resist doing.

_____

_____

_____

_____

2. Next, write down something your child likes to do that might logically come after this activity, or occurs regularly anyway.

_____

_____

_____

_____

Now, use these answers above to fill in the blanks on the next page:

When you have:

_____

_____

_____

_____

Then you may:

_____

_____

_____

_____

or if you:

_____

_____

_____

_____

Then you may:

_____

_____

_____

_____

Try this, and see how it goes. Remember to stay direct and calm, and be willing to let the consequences follow. Make sure to express appreciation if they do the thing that was asked.

Chapter Eleven

A Master Class

Jesus mastered teaching during His earthly ministry. His power to teach and help people change came from the way He lived His life. He was obedient to His Father and did all that He was commanded to do. He was the perfect example of one who is compassionate, forgiving, and patient, along with many other wonderful attributes. But the one that was at the heart of everything He did was love. Whether He was encouraging a penitent sinner, tutoring His disciples, or questioning a Pharisee, everything the Savior did expressed love. This love and compassion for people led Him to teach in meaningful ways. When the Savior taught, familiar, real-life experiences like fishing and herding sheep became spiritual lessons.

Teaching in the Savior's way means we will do what we can to be like Jesus. Our actions can then speak louder than our words. Others will remember the truths we share because they are evident in us. Our example can be a powerful influence on the attitudes of those around us. Being approachable and showing love helps us to connect. Our words and actions combine to create a safe place for people to learn and grow. We can look to Jesus Christ to know how to do these things. He is our best teacher.

Jesus Is Our Light

In John 8:12 says, "Then spake Jesus again unto them, saying, I am the light of the world: he that followeth me shall not walk in darkness, but shall have the light of life." Jesus came into the world to be the light to the world. His example shows us the way. We will be blessed when we learn of Him so that we might try to be like Him.

Matthew 5:14-16 reads, "Ye are the light of the world. A city that is set on an hill cannot be hid. Neither do men light a candle, and put it under a bushel, but on a candlestick; and it giveth light unto all that are in the house. Let your light so shine before men, that they may see your good works, and glorify your Father which is in heaven." We learn that we can be a light to the world. It is up to us to let our light shine. We are called to share the news that He is the way. We send this message to others by how we live our lives.

Interestingly, the candlestick that we put the light on is to bring light to all those in our house, which suggests that we should first share our light with those in our own house. We can make sharing His light with our family members our priority. Jesus is the light we can hold up so that others may know to come to Him. His light shines through us and guides our actions in how we choose to live our lives. We can create a house where the light of Christ is present by walking in His ways.

Jesus Is Relatable

Jesus taught using things that were relatable to the people He was hoping to reach. When He spoke to fishermen, He talked about fish. When He spoke to others, He spoke of sheep and water and things they understood. What things are your children interested in? How can you relate your "lessons" to their interests?

Jesus taught individuals lessons. His lessons were personal and timely, and had a way of lifting those who had ears to hear. The woman at the well was someone the Savior reached.[102] Not only did Jesus use something very relatable to this Samaritan woman, but He used a common everyday event to help her have a desire to understand His words. His comments about water caught her interest, and she wanted to know more. We can do likewise. This woman came to this well every day to get water and was surprised that Jesus would ask her for a drink, let alone strike up a conversation with her because she was a Samaritan. Jews and Samaritans were supposed to be enemies. Do you think she ever looked at water in the same way? The Savior's words and love helped her to change. Our words also have the power to influence others.

When we have moments like this with our loved ones, we can pray for eyes to see opportunities to show love and teach those in our care. It doesn't have to be big. It is better if they are small, simple matters. We just have to learn to see them for what they are: opportunities to teach. Being distracted may cause us to miss opportunities to be a light. Jesus prayed for opportunities. We can do this as well.

---

102   John 4:6-30.

The other day I was in the store and a four-year-old boy kicked over a stack of toilet paper rolls. He did this with one karate chop. Impressive! I was curious what the mom would do. She gently stopped and asked him to stack the toilet paper rolls again. He, of course, wanted to know why he had to pick them up. She asked him who had knocked it over. When he remembered it was him, he said, "It was me, so I should clean it up, huh?" After he did so, I may have thanked the mom for being a good adult. I love seeing parents taking the time to teach. (It took less than 30 seconds!)

One last thought on making our lessons relatable. When we focus on the person and not the lesson we hope to teach, we can be an instrument in the Lord's hand. We have to be careful that we don't get so fixated on teaching a lesson that we forget the needs of the individual. Jesus expressed love for those He taught. He understood it was much more than presenting a lesson. It was ministering with love. We can do likewise if we focus on the needs of those around us and not on our need to tell a good story, make a good point, or lecture a child in the grocery store. Keep it short and simple. With practice, we can learn to teach as He did.

Even Lawyers Have a Hard Time Arguing with Themselves

In Luke 10:25-28, Jesus gives a lawyer a chance to think for himself when he tries to tempt Jesus saying, "Master, what shall I do to inherit eternal life?" The lawyer is trying to trick Jesus into arguing with him. To avoid arguing, Jesus turns the question back on the lawyer. "What is written in the law? how readest thou?" The lawyer answers back correctly by saying, "Thou shalt love the Lord thy God with all thy heart, and with all thy soul, and with all thy strength, and with all thy mind; and thy neighbour as thyself." If Jesus had answered the lawyers question, the lawyer may have tried to argue with Jesus. But because Jesus lets the lawyer answer there is no argument. It is hard to argue with yourself. This lawyer understands the written law and is only trying to trick Jesus. Letting the lawyer answer his own question takes the thunder out of his argument. Jesus is then able to teach deeper truths about who our neighbors are after the lawyer is ready to learn.

Our children sometimes act like this lawyer. They want to argue their point. Turning their questions back on them makes it hard for them to argue. For instance, if a child wants to attend a concert you are not comfortable with, he may say something like, "Why won't you let me go?" You could say, "Why do you think I might not want you to go to this concert?"

The teen may try to get the parent off track by saying something like, "You just don't understand. I really want to go." They will typically try to get you off track three times.[103] If you continue to ask the same question, they might think for themselves about why the concert was inappropriate. They may actually list some of the inappropriate things about the concert. Having it come from them is more powerful than you listing inappropriate things about the concert. When it comes from them, they can see for themselves why it wouldn't be a good idea to go. Being calm like the Savior is another thing that can help us influence our children. (We'll cover this character trait in Chapter Thirteen.)

Jesus asked questions to invite learners to think deeply about important truths. Our questions to our loved ones can also inspire them to think deeply. An inspired question can help individuals think for themselves and feel new truths forming in their own minds instead of being told what to believe. Inspired questions make learning more engaging and personally meaningful. It also helps parents know what their children understand. Parents can identify and correct misunderstandings and learn what they still need to teach.

This may have been one reason Jesus asked others questions. He wanted to see what they already understood so that He could cater their learning experience to the level they were ready for. We can avoid issues in communication if we gauge where our children are before we launch into a big explanation. If a child asks where babies come from, we can ask them what they think. This helps us avoid the awkward "talk" if they just want reassurance about babies coming from heaven. Clarifying questions can help us dodge bullets and meet the learning needs of our children.

Jesus Understood How to Reach the People He Was Teaching

Jesus met the needs of His learners. He could adjust how He taught depending on who He was teaching. For instance, Jesus understood Peter and loved him greatly. In John 21:15-17, we get to see a teaching moment the Savior had with Peter. Jesus asked Peter to feed his sheep three times. Jesus knew Peter and knew how to reach him. Repeating the same question three times is significant and impactful. Sometimes we need to hear things more than once for the message to sink in. Peter was so set on what he hoped was obvious that he missed what Jesus was asking him to do. Jesus knew Peter loved Him, but He needed Peter to focus on feeding His sheep.

---

103   Latham, 2002.

Repeating His question three times helped Peter concentrate on what was important. It helps us make sure that we are understood and not misunderstood. We may have to say the same thing three times, or break down our message into smaller bites to help the listener understand. A simple way to do this is to have children repeat back what you said. This lets you know what they understood. If we follow Jesus's example, we can be clearer with the messages we are sending our loved ones.

When our oldest was small, she was very inquisitive. She was thirsty for knowledge and was always asking "why" (maybe you know someone like this). By the end of the day, the number of questions she asked exhausted me. One question led to another and another. I felt I had to keep going deeper with each question she asked.

We were visiting some childhood friends, and my friend's father was working in his garden. My daughter went over to him and started asking questions. She asked questions like, "Why is the sky blue?" "Why is that worm chubby?" "Why is that plant so green?" I listened to the simple truthful answers he gave her, like, "The sky is blue because God made it that way." She restated the same question, and he patiently said the same answer. I thought I needed to go deeper with each question, and all she needed was simple truths repeated. Simple truths about God gave her peace of mind. Her questions were not as tiring after that (most days). I still had to go deeper now and then, but it wasn't constant like it had been. Her quest for knowledge continued, but I knew how to respond. It takes time for the truth to sink in.

I realized this also has an application when our kids try to get out of doing something they don't want to do. They may say, "I don't want to clean my room!" Your simple response can be, "I'm glad you understand your room needs to be cleaned." Then, when they restate their resistance to cleaning, stating the task again will help them understand what they are being asked. It usually only takes three times for them to realize what we expect. We don't have to get louder to make a point. We just need to restate the request three times for our expectations to sink in. This is a gentler way than getting frustrated and yelling. Jesus showed us the way, even in this simple yet powerful teaching tool. I am grateful for His example in all things.

On-Call Teaching

Jesus invited us to become like Him, and one of His great attributes is His ability to teach. He is the Master Teacher. To become like Him, we too need to become more loving and life-changing teachers, not only at church but also in our homes. To become like Him, we ought to have a burning desire in our hearts to teach as He taught.

- Tad A. Callister, John S. Tanner, Devin G. Durrant[104]

In this quote, we are reminded that Jesus is the Master Teacher. We can become more like Him when we teach as He taught.

Parental teaching is like being an on-call physician. We always need to be ready to teach our children because we never know when the opportunity will present itself. We are like the Savior, who's teaching often did not happen in a synagogue but in informal, every-day settings—while eating a meal with His disciples, drawing water from a well, or walking past a fig tree.[105]

Elder Devin G. Durrant reminds us we are always "on call." Our children need us to be ready to teach when they are ready to learn. What do you hope your children are learning from you?

Some of our best teaching moments happen when we are busy living life, but we have to be careful not to be too busy or too distracted to see opportunities to teach. Listen to their voiced and unvoiced questions. Be curious enough to find out what they are thinking and feeling as you walk along a country road or as you are driving. Ask children things like, "Why do you have such a big grin on your face?" or "When do you think it will snow?" Questions start us down the road to discovery and allow us to share the world around us. These informal settings lend themselves to teaching and sharing love.

My dad shared sunsets with me. Some nights were silent, focused on the color in the sky, but other nights we talked about our day. Once in a while, he'd give me glimpses of his feelings about deeper things. "Sunsets remind me God is in charge, and looking at this one I feel loved." I still feel loved every time I look at a sunset. Such a simple thing. The gentle smiles he wore as he looked at sunsets made me wonder if he was thinking about and feeling God's love. Since he passed away about a year ago, sunsets have become even more tender for me. Some of our best teaching happens when we are just sharing our thoughts or listening to theirs. It doesn't have to be complicated. Simple things can lift and inspire.

---

104 Tad A. Callister, John S. Tanner, Devin G. Durrant, "What Manner of Teachers Ought We To Be," *Liahona*, January 2015.

105 Devin G. Durrant, "Teaching in the Home-A Joyful and Sacred Responsibility," *Ensign*, May 2018.

One last thought on teaching. Steven Sharp Nelson, the cellist in the Piano Guys, lost his dad last year too. I love what he said about his dad, "My Dad never preached at me, but he was a beautiful teacher of testimony. Do you know how he taught me? He loved Jesus so much in front of me I couldn't help but pick up on it."[106] This is something we can strive to do. We can love Jesus in front of our kids so they know where our peace and joy come from. It is often not what we say, but who we are that speaks the loudest. Our children can know Jesus Christ by watching us attempt to walk in His ways.

Teaching vs. Punishing

Some of our greatest parenting concerns are about how to discipline our children. We wonder how much is too much and how much is too little. We wonder if what we are doing will help or hinder our children's growth. These questions cause us to ponder how we should discipline our children. Disciplining children can be overwhelming. We feel responsible for teaching them right from wrong, but too often, discipline means punishment. Is punishing our children the best way to discipline them? Do we have to punish them to teach important lessons? Questions like these plague many parents! But let's break it down.

Let's start with the word "discipline." What does it mean? Discipline comes from the Latin root word, "disciplina" which means to instruct, teach, or train. It can mean to punish, but it does not have to. When we discipline children, we can concentrate on effective ways to teach them instead of ways to punish them. How does this change parenting for us? According to parent educator Glenn Latham:

> When a child misbehaves, that is evidence the child has either not been taught to behave properly, or the child is more often reinforced for behaving inappropriately than for behaving appropriately. Therefore, inappropriate behavior must be recognized as an opportunity to teach, not an excuse to punish. Punishment is no answer, it's an excuse.[107]

So how do we teach our children? In Proverbs 22:6, we learn, "Train up a child in the way he should go: and when he is old, he will not depart from it." This scripture reminds us to teach our children the things they should do. There are many ways to do this, but studies have shown that the most

---

106 Steve Sharp Nelson, *Turning Crisis into Crescendo: Using the Power of Creativity and Grace*, LDSPMA Conference, October 2023.

107 Dr. Glenn L. Latham, *The Power of Positive Parenting*, (Logan: P&T Ink, 1993), 6.

effective way to teach children is to be positive. Show them the right way to go and emphasize when they are doing the right thing, which will reinforce good choices. This is where we can put our focus instead of on their mistakes. (For more discussion and insights on how to do this, go to Chapter Five on being positive.)

Discipline does not need to be seen as punishment. Throughout this book, there have been examples of the Savior showing us the way we can teach and treat our children. Take the time to be intentional and you will be led to truth and light when you turn to Him. We are given opportunities to teach every day. This does not need to stress us out or make us nervous. We can look to the Savior and "watch" how He taught others. His humble approach to teaching is inspiring. He listened, loved, and shared. We can do this! He loves us and will be our guide.

Intentional Teaching

Workbook

Have you ever wondered what distinguishes families that thrive from those that flounder? Neither type of family is immune to issues. All families have struggles! The difference is in the way families respond to these problems.

We may need to look at problems in a new way to not flounder when they come. If we look at problems as opportunities to teach children important things like responsibility, courage, cooperation, and important skills like problem-solving, conflict resolution, and even cooperation, then maybe the problems are not so horrible after all. They may be a tool we can use to prepare our children for the world they live in. Learning to face problems gives us a chance to help our children not only survive but thrive in the world around them. Without problems, we may not be given opportunities to teach our children all they need to know.

Jesus did not tiptoe around touchy subjects. He went out on many proverbial limbs to help those around Him understand a better way of living. He questioned the Pharisees about their interpretations of the laws of Moses [108] Are there any "touchy subjects" that have been avoided to keep the

---

108   Matthew 22:34-40.

peace in your home? Are there messy rooms that are ignored? Is there a time of day when people seem to disappear to avoid jobs? Is there some work no one wants to do? Is there something your child should do on his own and you just haven't taken the time to teach him or her?

During the week, observe your family and write out some problems or issues you can see. Are these opportunities for you to teach your child/children a new skill or a useful life lesson?

1. What are some problems you see in your home?

_____

_____

_____

_____

2. Is there something a child is capable of doing on their own, but you haven't taken the time to teach them yet?

_____

_____

_____

_____

3. Choose one of these problems to address:

_____

_____

_____

_____

4. What are the qualities or skills you could teach?

_____

_____

_____

_____

5. How will you teach this skill?

_____

_____

_____

_____

6. Will you work side by side with a child? Or will you give them a task and follow up after they have completed the task?

_____

_____

_____

_____

7. How will you make sure they know how to do the job?

_____

_____

_____

_____

8. Will you model the way to do the job? How?

_____

_____

_____

_____

9. Will you give them a chance to show you they are capable of the work you are asking them to do?

_____

_____

_____

_____

10. How will you show acceptance of what they can do?

_____

_____

_____

_____

11. How will you show you value them and the job they have completed?

_____

_____

_____

_____

12. What will you challenge them with next?

_____

_____

_____

_____

Here are some intentional things we can ask ourselves to help us be better teachers to our children:

1. I can show my love for my family members by:

_____

_____

_____

_____

2. I have gotten to know them by:

_____

_____

_____

3. I take an interest in them by:

_____

_____

_____

_____

4. I focus my prayers on my family by:

_____

_____

_____

_____

5. I minister to them by:

_____

_____

_____

6. I am teaching them to love and serve others by:

_____

_____

_____

_____

7. I watch over them by:

_____

_____

_____

_____

Chapter Twelve

Tears for Breakfast

Now for the chapter where we put it all together. We are finally going to explore how to stay calm when there is chaos erupting upstairs, downstairs, and everywhere in between. We'll look to the Savior for the answers we seek.

The Savior relied on His inner strength to stay courageously calm when faced with challenges. Our inner strength and His example can help us similarly. If we humble ourselves and seek His will, He can guide us. The wonderful thing about seeking Him is that He is patient with us as we learn. I know this from personal experience.

The following is one of my lowest moments as a parent, and I'm embarrassed to share my mistakes. The arrival of our third child left me feeling stressed and overwhelmed. (I think it had something to do with the fact that I had more children than arms, and growing another arm was not an option!) My circumstances humbled me and caused me to ask hard questions and seek answers. I found the answers in the attributes of the Savior. I learned better ways of dealing with my frustration, anger, and feelings of being overwhelmed. I hope you can find relatable truths to help you face your challenges and see how the attributes we've studied come together. I invite you to join me for breakfast, where tears are the main course.

Tears for Breakfast

I can't believe I yelled at my son for spilling milk. It happened so quickly. The milk jug just slipped out of my five-year-old's hands. What a mess! Both he and the floor were covered in milk, and I was frustrated. My daughter sensed the tension and rushed from the room in tears. My baby's wails rang out. The milk spiller was in a state of shock and scared of what I would do next. They were upset because I was yelling again.

I shouldn't have lost my temper over spilled milk. The saying "Don't cry over spilled milk" came to mind, reminding me that no amount of crying (or yelling) would return milk to the container. I was more worried about the words I could never get back. I wondered what would happen in the future if I hollered about insignificant, accidental things like this. Telling myself not to yell wasn't enough. I didn't want to serve tears for breakfast, but what could I do?

The milk incident was still weighing on my heart four days later on Sunday. During a Sunday School lesson, we discussed the woman caught in adultery who was brought to the Savior. I had always concentrated on the Savior's compassionate response to the woman. But this time it was the way He dealt with the judgmental scribes and Pharisees that caught my attention. How did Jesus stay calm? This question stayed with me for the rest of the day.

During a quiet moment, I read John 8:1-11 and let the scene play out in my mind. I could see the serene setting near the temple where the Savior was teaching. Visualizing the commotion the scribes and Pharisees created as they brought the sobbing woman to Jesus made my heart ache. I wondered if they were shouting to show the level of disdain they felt for her. The difference between how the Savior responded and how the scribes and Pharisees handled this situation was notable.

The scribes and Pharisees were ready to argue and came pointing their fingers at the woman to stir up trouble. I have to admit the scribes and Pharisees reminded me of my kids when they accused their siblings of something or tried to get out of a chore. Jesus didn't let the actions of the scribes and Pharisees determine how He would respond. He decided to intentionally respond in positive, calm ways instead of reacting in anger. Jesus didn't react. He acted.

We choose how we act when confronted, disappointed, frustrated, or caught off guard. One of Satan's cunning lies is to dissociate anger from agency, making us feel we are victims of an emotion we cannot control. When we say, "I lost my temper," it implies we were not responsible. Someone else "made" us mad, but that is just not true. Becoming angry is a conscious choice. No one can "make" us angry. We choose to become that way. Jesus understood this and gave us an example to follow.

I love the way John describes the Savior's actions. ". . . Jesus stooped down, and with his finger wrote on the ground, as though he heard them not."[109] I can picture the scene the scribes and Pharisees were making. They

---

109   John 8:6.

were so busy shouting accusations about the woman that they could not listen. Jesus understood this and didn't shout over them. He waited for them to be quiet. When Jesus ignored them, it made it seem their outburst did not affect Him. This was not the reaction they expected. And so in their stunned, quiet state, His simple words were then enough to teach, "He that is without sin among you, let him first cast a stone. "[110]

Staying calm during the outbursts of others is hard to do, but it can dispel anger quickly. My former Bishop, Dr. Glenn Latham, did research on this Christlike approach. He states, "I have been astounded to find that if parents remain calm, empathetic, and direct even in the face of outrageous reviling, 97 out of 100 times, on the third directive, children will comply."[111] It amazes me how consistently my children's anger disappears after their third attempt to engage me in an argument. If I stay calm their anger goes away.

Another thing I realized is that Jesus didn't just decide to be calm when problems arose. He took time to pray, reflect, ponder, and center Himself often. This may have been why He went to the Mount of Olives before going to the temple.[112] He was intentional in the way He lived His life. When Jesus woke in the morning, He didn't know angry men would confront Him while He was teaching (at least I don't think He did), but He could deliberately choose how He would respond. When we take time to center ourselves, we will act with more purpose instead of reacting to the current conditions around us. Christ's prayers to His Father prepared Him to face the challenges of His day.

My prayers led me to inspect my daily interactions with my family. I took notes on how things went for a few days. I looked at what went well and the times we struggled. Journaling in this way helped me to be objective. Instead of just getting stuck feeling bad, I looked for solutions. I also realized that I was not a complete failure as a mother. There were many bright spots in our day.

It surprised me to discover that our trouble spots often occurred at the same time and were about the same things. I decided to "fix" our trouble spots so they didn't trouble us anymore. The Lord prompted me to make some intentional changes, like establishing a nightly routine that helped everyone know what to expect. A healthy snack in the afternoon made it so there were fewer tears before dinner. When milk spilled at breakfast, I learned to take a deep breath, say a quick prayer, and picture the Savior in the moment before I responded. This helped me to stay calm and in control of my actions (most of the time). Working through these trouble spots made it easier to be calm.

---

110   John 8:7.
111   Dr. Glenn L. Latham, *Christlike Parenting*, (Seattle: Gold Leaf Press, 2002), 69.
112   John 8:1.

Focusing on expressing love and ignoring some inconsequential behaviors helped me to train my eyes to see the good in my family members.

Since studying this bible story, yelling seemed like a lazy way to parent. I had developed the mistaken belief that yelling was a necessary part of parenting because it seemed to get immediate results. I realized that in the long run, my lack of self-control could cause anger and resentment to build in my children and possibly cause my teenagers to rebel. I could quell this by simply staying calm and not abusing my power.

As I continued to study, I realized that Jesus loved the scribes and Pharisees. I had overlooked this. These contentious men were also God's children. Jesus was sent to earth to give everyone a chance to return to the Father. Jesus was patient and looked for the best way to reach them. I could let the love I have for my children help me be patient. With God's help, I could reach them.

It surprised me that His love and compassion were the keys to the Savior's ability to stay calm. Just imagine how scared and embarrassed the woman caught in adultery must have been. Jesus understood this. When we are compassionate, we try to feel what others may be feeling and consider how we would want to be treated. This softens our hearts so we can respond with empathy instead of anger.

Jesus showed compassion by taking the focus off the woman. He asked her accusers the following, ". . . He that is without sin among you, let him first cast a stone at her."[113] Jesus gave them some time to reflect while He bent down and continued writing in the dirt. His question was something the men couldn't argue with, and they went off. Jesus then knelt near the woman and asked her some questions. Jesus reproved in private and praised in public. This is something I could do with my children.

Jesus remained compassionate despite the scribes and Pharisees trying to get Him off track. It's easy to get off track when children are yelling, screaming, or throwing a tantrum. The key is to stay focused on the actual issue. Jesus stayed focused and ignored the noise. He could then discuss important principles with those around Him.

The Jewish interpretations of the Mosaic laws of the time were very harsh and didn't encourage compassion or redemption. This law about adultery had not been enforced in this way for hundreds of years. For these men to insist on stoning the woman shows their desire to put Jesus in a tricky spot. Jesus was known for His compassion, and they wanted to test Him to see if He would uphold the law. Jesus showed concern for her suffering

---

113   John 8:7.

and took action to help. He did not congratulate the accusers for finding someone sinning. Instead, Jesus asked the men to consider their own hearts. This perfectly timed, humble inquiry allowed them to reflect inwardly. Jesus then encouraged the woman to change. ". . . Woman, where are those thine accusers? hath no man condemned thee? She said, "No man, Lord. And Jesus said unto her, "Neither do I condemn thee: go, and sin no more.""[114]

Condemnation would not have helped this woman to change, but the Savior knew that love could. His response to her sinfulness was wonderful because it was about progression and the ability He gives all of us to repent, turn to Him, and move on. The scribes and Pharisees were looking for a chance to punish. Jesus chose to lift, teach, and forgive. How effective was His teaching? The Joseph Smith Translation of the Bible gives us the rest of her story. It says, ". . . And the woman glorified God from that hour, and believed on his name"[115] Here, love brought about lasting change.

What could I do to bring about lasting change? Jesus lovingly questioned those He hoped to influence. His questions gave people a chance to focus on their own actions instead of the actions of others. The accusers went away, and Jesus was able to question her without an audience. I could ask my children better questions instead of telling them what they should or shouldn't be doing. I could do this quietly and calmly, without an audience. I needed to remember to praise in public and reprove in private. Giving children the responsibility of thinking about their own actions can bring about lasting change.

The milk incident happened over twenty years ago, and I am still trying to master being calm. Once in a while, the "yeller" returns, but I have made progress. I have learned to humbly view the times I get upset as opportunities to grow instead of an excuse to feel bad. Cutting the yelling out of my day was a conscious, gradual process that was freeing, and worth the effort. With the example and help of Jesus Christ, I now see contentious moments as times to teach instead of an excuse to punish. The following was a recent conversation that gave my heart peace:

> One of my daughters had an early volleyball tournament. My youngest was having a rough morning and took it out on me. She yelled about having to go so early. She complained about not being able to find her "stupid" socks and having to go to her sister's "stupid" tournament. During all this, I chose to stay calm and compassionate. I didn't argue with her or try to fix her thinking or even the "stupid" words she used. I thought little of it until

---

114   John 8:10-11.
115   JST John 8:11.

a few days later when we were driving in the car together and we had the following conversation.

"So, Mom, have you noticed that I have been nicer to you?"

"Yes . . . thank you," I hadn't noticed anything significant, but if she felt she was making an effort to be nicer, I would not complain. I asked her, "Have you been trying to be nicer?"

She smiled and said, "Yes, I realized I could do better. I'm sorry, I kinda forgot Saturday morning. I was really ornery."

I smiled my forgiveness and said, "I'm sorry we had to leave so early. It was tough for me as well."

"Mom, why didn't you yell back?" she said hesitantly.

"Mmm, I'm trying to be more like Jesus. He had people yelling at Him all the time, but He didn't yell back. Did you know Jesus had men get angry with Him because He healed someone on Sunday? And yet He stayed calm," I said.

"How did He do that?" she asked.

"Well, Jesus didn't let their ranting change how He was going to act. He chose to be calm instead of reacting in anger."

"Mom, you did that the other morning. I was really ornery, and you stayed calm . . . I think I can do that, too," she said.

The Savior's example of staying calm to teach inspires. His controlled response was effective with the scribes and Pharisees. His example has also helped me with toddlers throwing temper tantrums and angry teenagers. When we respond as the Savior did, we not only become more like Him, but we invite others to feel His love and follow Him. We also feel the joy that only comes from following Him.

Thank you for joining me for breakfast. I've been able to improve what I serve my family over the years thanks to the great tutor, Jesus Christ. I still burn the toast and undercook the eggs, but things are getting better. The Savior and my family are patient as I learn. I hope you can learn from my mistakes so you can avoid making similar ones. But if you also serve tears for breakfast, lunch, or dinner, don't lose hope! The Savior's example is for everyone! The workbook will give you a chance to apply His example to things you have cooking at home. Know that you are loved and can work through your challenges.

Intentional Calmness

Workbook

1. How can we learn to act instead of allowing ourselves to be acted upon?

_____

_____

_____

_____

2. Who is in charge of our anger? Why does this matter?

_____

_____

_____

_____

3. How did the Savior's quiet approach affect the scribes and Pharisees?

_____

_____

_____

_____

4. Do you think staying calm and empathetic will help dispel anger when you are confronted? Why or why not? Are you willing to see if it only takes three times to dispel anger?

_____

_____

_____

_____

5. What things did the Savior do to be intentional about His day? What helps to center you?

_____

_____

_____

_____

6. How do the attributes of love and compassion help us be calm?

_____

_____

_____

_____

7. How did the questions Jesus asked help those involved stay focused on their own actions?

_____

_____

_____

_____

8. How can we make contentious moments opportunities to teach?

_____

_____

_____

_____

9. What was your biggest takeaway from this account?

_____

_____

_____

_____

Troubleshooting Our Day

Can troubleshooting our day help us stay calm? The answer is YES!!! Many are overwhelmed with all that life throws at us. This section encourages you to look at the trouble spots in your day and work through them. This gives you a chance to be intentional and possibly avoid relying on your anger to "solve" your problems.

Many of us deal with the same trouble spots day in and day out. Our kids throw temper tantrums about the same things at about the same time of day repeatedly. By looking at our trouble spots and working through them, we can avoid many of them. If we plan to be calm, then there is a greater chance we will be calm. Roll up your sleeves, and let's get to work.

1. Look at your day objectively for a few days and make note of when you feel contention in your home.
2. When you are calm, prayerfully look over your notes. See if there are any patterns in your children's behavior, or when you struggle to be calm. Do you see more meltdowns right before dinner? Do you struggle more when your kids are trying to do their homework?
3. Tackle one area at a time. Move on when you feel better about your trouble spot.

4. Be patient with yourself and others. It takes time to work through your trouble spots, but once you get going in the right direction, it will move faster than you think. The Lord will bless your efforts and magnify them. Remember, the Lord loves effort and likes it when we do hard things.

Here is a chart to help you trouble shoot your day. The questions walk you through the process of fixing your trouble spots.

Trouble Spot

Look at your day and find the times or things that make it hard to stay calm.	What makes it hard for you to stay calm? Name it	**Plan ahead** What can you change about the situation? See questions below.	What would the Savior do in this situation? Instead of reacting, how can you act?	Teach expectations, use consequences, and redirect inappropriate behavior.
Example: 10:30 Kids fight over toys	I don't like contention. It makes me anxious.	Establish a plan for taking turns and practice doing this. Do this when we are all calm.	I think Jesus would wait until they were calm, show compassion, and instill courage in them to do better.	Gently remind them how to ask for a toy. Calmly practice sharing and acknowledge their efforts.
Mornings				
Afternoons				
Evenings				

Questions to Ask Yourself as You Troubleshoot Your Day

1. Am I acting like a dictator, or am I letting others "walk all over me"?

2. Can I ignore the problem behavior and wait to "catch 'em bein' good"?

3. Can the problem area be fixed if I change something physical?

    Ex. Put sugary sweets out of sight and reach of children.

    Ex. Set out Sunday shoes the night before.

4. Could a procedure be put in place, so the kids know what is expected of them?

    Ex. Have clothes on before they eat breakfast.

5. Have I taught them what is expected of them?

    Ex. After dinner, everyone disappears, and I am stuck cleaning up the mess. If everyone understood they were expected to help clean the kitchen, then I wouldn't be stuck cleaning everything myself. Could this be discussed during Family Council?

6. Am I doing too much or too little for them?

7. Am I discouraging or encouraging my child?

8. Am I giving the child/children freedom within limits?

9. Am I having a power struggle with my child/children? By giving them a choice, can I dispel the struggle?

10. Am I giving them credit and recognizing their efforts?

11. Am I talking respectfully to my children?

12. Am I distracted instead of paying attention to their needs?

    Ex. Phone, TV, Computer, etc.

13. How is my tone of voice? Too soft, too loud, too sarcastic? Firm, but loving? How does my tone of voice affect the children?

Chapter Thirteen

Courage to Take the Next Right Step

Let's explore what it means to be courageous. It can mean different things to different people. We're not going to get into some things the world today finds courageous, but instead, focus on what "Christlike Courage" looks like. Lynn G. Robbins said, "Courage is not just one of the cardinal virtues, but as C. S. Lewis observed: 'Courage is . . . the form of every virtue at the testing point.'"[116]

The best example of someone who is truly courageous is Jesus Christ. We have seen His virtues at the testing point, and He has always chosen to be courageous. He met every test He faced head-on. The scriptures give us a glimpse of how He showed forgiveness, charity, and compassion; and how he offered mercy to others. We can witness His courage because He was tested and tried in every way. And sometimes, in every way possible, all at once. He truly has shown us how to have courage and be faithful to Heavenly Father.

Soon after His baptism the Savior's courage was tested by Satan. The Spirit led Jesus into the wilderness, where He remained for forty days and nights, preparing Himself for His formal ministry, which was soon to begin. During this time, He chose to fast so that He might be closer to His Father.[117] When Jesus completed His fast, He was hungry and in a physically weakened state. And yet this was the very hour Satan tempted Him. (Of course, Satan sure knows when to strike!)

Satan's first temptation was to entice Jesus to satisfy His craving for food. "If thou be the Son of God, command that these stones be made bread."[118]

---

116   Lynn G. Robbins, "Which Way Do You Face," *Liahona*, October 2014.
117   Matthew 4:1-12.
118   Matthew 4:3.

Satan was not simply tempting Jesus to eat. Had he suggested, "Go down out of this wilderness and obtain food from the bread maker," there would have been no temptation. Undoubtedly, Jesus intended to eat. The temptation was in the invitation to turn stones into bread miraculously so He wouldn't have to wait to eat. He'd have instant gratification instead. His reply to the tempter was crystal clear: "It is written, Man shall not live by bread alone, but by every word that proceedeth out of the mouth of God."[119]

The second temptation took place on the top of the temple, overlooking the spacious courts and people below. Satan tempted Jesus by saying, "If Thou be the Son of God, cast thyself down: for it is written, He shall give his angels charge concerning thee: and in their hands they shall bear thee up."[120] If Jesus was unhurt by this feat, He would receive public recognition. It would be a sign and a wonder, the fame of which would spread like wildfire throughout all of Judaea and cause many to believe the Messiah had indeed come. But Jesus didn't seek fame or recognition. He sought to fulfill the will of His Father. Jesus once more thwarted Satan's plan when He said, "It is written again, thou shalt not tempt the Lord thy God."[121]

In his third temptation, Satan showed Jesus all the kingdoms of the world. With wealth, splendor, and earthly glory spread before them, Satan said unto him, "All these things will I give thee, if thou wilt fall down and worship me."[122] In power and dignity, Jesus commanded, "Get thee hence, Satan: for it is written, Thou shalt worship the Lord thy God, and him only shalt thou serve."[123] Defeated, Satan turned and went away. "And when the devil had ended all the temptation," Luke adds, "he departed from him for a season."[124] Jesus was tempted three times by Satan and, because Jesus stayed calm, Satan went away defeated. It appears that instead of being weakened by fasting, Jesus was strengthened.

When the tests came, Jesus was courageous and resisted all the temptations placed before Him. The Joseph Smith Translation adds one other way that the Savior was courageous. Heavenly Father sent angels to minister to Jesus, but Jesus sent these comforting angels to John the Baptist who had just been put in prison.[125] Jesus put other people's needs before His own even during this testing point. There is still a bit more from Matthew 4:12, which says, "he departed into Galilee." This suggests that Jesus got started on the

---

119   Matthew 4:4.
120   Matthew 4:6.
121   Matthew 4:7.
122   Matthew 4:9.
123   Mathew 4:10.
124   Luke 4:13.
125   JT Matthew 4:11-12.

work He was sent to do. Isn't this revealing and wonderful? He didn't want to waste any time.

We can be courageous and follow the example of Jesus Christ by having courage during our testing points. We can recognize things that tempt us and work to avoid these enticements. All that we may be tempted with today could fall into one of these three categories: First, a temptation of appetite. Second, a temptation that appeals to our vanity or pride. Third, a temptation that appeals to our desire for riches or power among men (or children). When these temptations come to us, we can have the courage to withstand them, even when the voices around us are taunting us. We can be strong and courageous, and hold true to who we are trying to become.

When we think of the courage the Savior has, we can be strengthened to meet our challenges head-on. He showed us how to live a life focused on Heavenly Father. Jesus loved His Father above all else. He showed us how to love, forgive, pray for, and serve our neighbors. He knows life will be tough, but He does not ask anything of us He is not willing to do Himself. He spent time with children even when He was tired. He showed compassion, healed the sick, and lifted burdens. He had the power to calm troubled seas, yet He did not use this power against those who wronged Him. He could have used this power to remove the bitter cup that only He could drink for all of us, but He did not do this.

His example encourages us to do better and be better. We can do what is required, and face our challenges because of Him. We can be loving, and take the time to show compassion. We can walk miles in the dust if necessary to ease someone's burdens. We can face hardships with love in our hearts, instead of anger toward God when things don't go our way. We can be calm because He was calm. We can forgive as He forgave. We can even be a parent in the latter days where wrong is right and right is wrong. We can do all of these things because we follow Jesus Christ!

We may stumble and make missteps, but we can be gentle with ourselves and others because He is gentle with us. He recognizes our efforts and knows our hearts. He knows we will not walk perfectly the first time, or the thirtieth time, and He will be there for us. He loves us and He will not leave us. His hands are stretched out still. Jesus dared to do His Father's will, and we can have courage to follow Him.

Think about the challenges you face as a parent and remember how Jesus faced His challenges with faith and courage. We truly can do likewise. When we are being tested, we can ask ourselves the age-old question, "What would Jesus do?" And it can help us in our moments of testing to have Christlike Courage!

Courage is at the heart of being a parent today from the initial decision to become a parent, to everything that follows. This decision is a big one and Satan knows it. He wants us to decide the problems we face are too large, and that we are not up to the challenge. We can face these challenges with courage because we can look to Christ. He can be with us every step of the way.

Courage is a parenting trait we can develop. It takes courage to be consistent and kind day in and day out, and to stay positive and calm when chaos is erupting around us. Study the Savior's actions and ponder on the courage the Savior must have had to do the difficult things He was asked to do. Ask yourself how His courage can help you to do hard things. How will it help you face discouragements and disappointments?

Fixes for Discouragement

We all get discouraged sometimes and it can be hard to work our way out of our discouragement. It takes courage to look at things with new eyes. Discouragement comes in all different shapes and sizes. Conquering parenting issues can feel good, but it is sometimes hard to know where to start. The following are some things that discourage parents, and some brief ways to work through the discouragements. For more help, don't hesitate to reach out to a professional. Here are a few things that can empower parents to overcome hard things:

- **Feeling Overwhelmed**: If you are feeling overwhelmed, look for non-essential things to cut out. Prioritize your priorities and do away with some of the "fluff." It is okay to do this. Don't try to run faster than you have strength. Look at how you use your time. If it is a really busy time, restructure your day and cut out some things that can be done during less busy times.

- **Getting stuck in the worry cycle**: It's easy to get consumed with worry. A simple way of handling this is to set a timer. Give yourself five minutes, or even ten minutes, to worry about a particular problem. When the timer goes off, move on to other things. During your worry time, write out the problem and write out possible solutions instead of letting the problem spin around in your head. This is one way to stop the spinning and get out of the worry cycle.

- **I messed up**: We all will, and that is okay. We can do better next time. We can stay calm instead of yelling. We can recognize the space between a stimulus and our response. Tomorrow is a new day.

Be humble. Ask for forgiveness and forgive yourself. Don't dwell on this mess-up. If you are discouraged, remind yourself of the successes you have had. List them. Don't dwell on your mess-ups.

• **Feelings of inadequacy**: This is one of Satan's oldest tricks. We all struggle with feelings of inadequacy. The trick is to simply move past it and not repeat the lies Satan is telling you. Instead, remind yourself that you did the best you could with what you knew at the time. You are enough and you are up to the challenges you face. Look to the Savior and study the ways He lived.

• **Feeling Alone:** Many of us feel alone in our parenting struggles. Reach out to others in a similar boat. You may be an answer to someone else's heartfelt prayer. Satan wants us to feel alone. Start a *Christ-Centered Intentional Parenting Group* in your area. Discuss Christ's example and your successes and mess-ups as you attempt to follow Him. There is strength in numbers. Share your burdens with others, and share them with the Lord. He will be there for you!

• **Problems seem too big**: Sometimes our problems feel too big. When they feel large, pick them apart. Write out the problem and then look for solutions. (Use the *Decision-Making Chart* found in Chapter Ten.) When it is on paper, it becomes a math problem. We don't have to be very emotional about math. We can just look at solving the problem and finding an answer. Using this approach to work through family issues is a great option. It helps individuals to avoid getting stuck just worrying about something.

• **I can't change**: Satan would have us believe that we can't change. You can't teach old dogs new tricks. But the truth is we can change, and we can look to the Savior for ways to be better. He really is the way (See Chapter Four on Forgiveness).

• **I'm not a perfect parent**: Let go of the worldly view of perfection and embrace Christ's view of working toward more completely loving and forgiving others, or any other of His wonderful attributes. Concentrate on Him and not on what the world deems perfect. He loves you and you are enough!

What Manner of Men Ought Ye to Be?

In 3 Nephi 27:27, Jesus posed a question that causes many to ponder: "Therefore, what manner of men ought ye to be?" Though He often leaves it up to us to find an answer to His questions, in this instance, Christ answers plainly, "Verily, I say unto you, even as I am." Through the example of His own life, Jesus shows us the way to live.

How do we become more like Him? How do we develop Christlike attributes? We study His life. His interactions show us the way we should treat those around us, especially our family members. The glimpses we get of Jesus as He interacts with people help us know how to forgive, listen, teach, and especially love others. He shows us how to meet people where they are. His calm actions not only helped others to be calm, but they were filled with compassion and forgiveness.

Looking to Jesus Christ can help us with even the toughest challenges we face in our families. He exemplified the love our Father in Heaven has for us. Jesus walked perfectly here on earth. We can get overwhelmed by the thought of striving to be like Him. Or we can take one step at a time and look to Him for the direction we should take. We truly can be perfected in Him.

The word "perfect" doesn't need to scare us. We know that we can work toward being more completely loving, forgiving, patient, and even calm because we have watched the Savior's sojourn here on earth. We know Heavenly Father sees our efforts to be more like His Son, and our hearts are lighter and may be filled with peace and even joy. We don't "earn" these feelings by "working" to do these things. They are by-products of striving to be like Him. These feelings help us to know that we are on the right track. It just makes things easier. Even parenting can be easier. Striving more completely to love others and more completely forgive others is something we can do. We know that studying the attributes of Jesus Christ can help us be more complete.

The thought of being courageous like Him may be overwhelming, but if we think of courage as just making the next right step we might not get as overwhelmed. Taking the next step is something we can do. As you have read this book, you may have taken steps towards being more like the Savior. Maybe you have been making positive changes in your family by making small intentional changes in your day, and because you had some success you decide to take the next right step. The momentum has kicked in, and it's easier to keep that forward motion going. You can make positive, impactful changes in one area of your day and feel the joy of doing this. Then other parts of your day can be affected similarly. It takes courage and effort to get heading in the right direction.

We know we can study and strive to be like Jesus our whole lives and still fall short, but that is okay. Jesus not only provides the perfect example for us to follow, He makes up the difference when we fall short. Striving to follow Jesus Christ brings peace. Studying His attributes can help us handle difficult situations in more Christlike, loving ways. Life is easier when we follow in His footsteps. He said, "my yoke is easy, and my burden is light."[126] Our burdens truly are made lighter when we strive to be like Him.

His love will sustain us, and His example will show the way. When we look to Him and learn of Him, our burdens will be lighter, our joy will increase, and those around us can feel His love through us. We have walked the dusty roads with Him, and have seen some ways He has interacted with others. In knowing Him, we can now strive to be more like Him. Jesus has shown us what manner of men we ought to be. We can have the courage to follow Him and do hard things. When we stumble and fall, we can get back up knowing that He will help us take the next right step because He loves us.

Just like He helped the Apostle Peter to walk on water, we can learn to put our focus on Jesus and look to Him in all things (even our parenting efforts). When we focus on Him, amazing things happen in our hearts and our lives. This focus helps our children to know where to look and who to follow. It helps us to reduce the amount of contention in our homes, and it helps us to feel peace and even joy in our hearts. This means a lot in the world we live in today.

The world may be in commotion, but in our families, we can have more peace because we are letting Jesus influence our lives. President Nelson said the following, "The Lord is gathering those who are willing to let God prevail in their lives. The Lord is gathering those who will choose to let God be the most important influence in their lives. For centuries, prophets have foretold this gathering, and it is happening right now! As an essential prelude to the Second Coming of the Lord, it is the most important work in the world!"[127] We can let God prevail in our lives.

In this book, we have focused on His attributes and learned more about Him and His ways. Knowing Him better allows us to try to be more like Him. The more we incorporate His actions into how we do things with our children, the more they can respond to us in similar ways. Our efforts to be more Christ-centered in our parenting can help us prepare for His Second coming. It can help our children know where to put their focus because it brings peace, joy, and light to an ever-darkening world.

---

126   Matthew 11:30.
127   Russell M. Nelson, "Let God Prevail," *Liahona*, October 2020.

Intentional Courageous Parenting

Workbook

A Closer Look at Courage

The Savior was intentional in the way He lived His life. He took time to reflect, ponder, and center Himself on His work. When we are humble and take the time to reflect and ponder (be intentional), we will act with more purpose instead of reacting to the current conditions around us. Let's take a closer look at the courage of the Savior. Ponder the questions below to be more courageous as a parent. It may surprise you how good it feels to know you are trying to follow in His footsteps.

1. How did Jesus show courage?

_____

_____

_____

_____

2. Why do you think these actions showed courage?

_____

_____

_____

_____

3. Who else from the scriptures inspires you to have courage? Why?

_____

_____

_____

_____

4. What things in your life take courage to face?

_____

_____

_____

_____

5. Which of your parenting dilemmas take courage to face? What attribute of the Savior will help you face this challenge?

_____

_____

_____

_____

6. How can the example of Jesus Christ help you to face your challenges?

_____

_____

_____

_____

7. What is your plan to face them?

_____

_____

_____

_____

8. What specific things can you do to have more Christlike courage?

_____

_____

_____

_____

_____

_____

_____

_____

Bibliography

Ballard, M. Russell, "Family Councils," *Ensign*, April 2016.

Caldwell, C. Max, "Love of Christ," *Ensign,* November 1992.

Clark, Kim B., "Look unto Jesus Christ," *Ensign,* May 2019.

Callister, Tad A., Tanner; John S., Durrant, Devin G., "What Manner of Teachers Ought We to Be," *Ensign,* January 2015.

Cordon, Bonnie H., Jones, Joy D. *"Intentional Parenting,"* BYU Women's Conference, 2017. https://www.byutv.org/4b69a304-e979-4c91-8a20-ab78752c34c8/byu-women's-conference-joy-d.-jones-and-bonnie-h.-cordon?q=joy%20d%20jones%20bonnie

Covey, Stephen R., *The 7 Habits of Highly Effective People: Powerful Lessons in Personal Change*, New York City: Simon and Schuster, 1999.

Eyring, Henry B., "A Home Where the Spirit of the Lord Dwells," *Ensign*, May 2019.

Faust, James E., "The Healing Power of Forgiveness," *Ensign,* May 2007.

Hales, Robert D., "Agency: Essential to the Plan of Life," *Ensign,* November 2010.

Hinckley, Gordon B., "The Continuing Pursuit of Truth," *Ensign,* May 1986.

——, "The Healing Power of Christ," *Ensign,* October 1988.

Knighton, Ronald L., "Becoming Our Children's Greatest Teachers," *Ensign*, September 1999.

Larson, Sharon G., "Agency- A Blessing and a Burden," *Ensign,* November 1999.

Latham, Glenn L., *Five Steps to Better Behavior,* Utah State University Married Stake Fireside, May 1994.

——, *Christlike Parenting,* Detroit: Gold Leaf Press, 2002.

——, *The Power of Positive Parenting,* Logan: P&T Ink, 1993.

——, *What's a Parent to Do?* Salt Lake City: Deseret Book, 1997.

Martino, James B., *Choose Ye This Day Whom Ye Will Serve,* BYU Devotional, September 15, 2020. https://speeches.byu.edu/talks/james-b-martino/choose-you-this-day-whom-ye-will-serve/

Maxwell, Neal A., *The Promise of Discipleship*, Salt Lake City: Deseret Book, 2001.

Merkley, Karen Rose, "Loaves, Fishes, and Compassion," *Ensign,* March 1995.

Monson, Thomas S., "Hidden Wedges," *Ensign,* May 2002.

Nelson, Russell M., "Drawing the Power of Jesus Christ into Our Lives," *Ensign,* May 2017.

——, "Joy and Spiritual Survival," *Ensign,* November 2016.

——, "Lessons from the Lord's Prayers," *Ensign,* May 2009.

——, "Peacemakers Needed," *Liahona,* May 2023.

——, "Spiritual Treasures," *Ensign,* November 2019.

——, "The Answer is Always Jesus Christ," *Liahona,* May 2023.

——, "We Can Do Better and Be Better," *Liahona,* May 2019.

Norton, Oak. "Principles of the Gospel of Jesus Christ and If/Then Logic." *Scripture Notes.* https://scripturenotes.com/principles-of-the-gospel-of-jesus-christ-and-if-then-logic Accessed Oct. 31, 2023.

Oaks, Dallin H., "The Atonement and Faith," *Ensign,* April 2010.

Oaks, Robert C., "The Power of Patience," *Ensign,* November 2006.

Palmer, Brent, Andrea, Palmer, "Worth of Souls Podcasts," http://www.youtube.com/@worthofsoulspodcast7259. Accessed 18 September 2023.

Popkin, Michael H., *Active Parenting: A Parent's Guide to Raising Happy and Successful Children,* Marietta: Active Parenting Publishers, 2014.

Popkin, Michael H., *Active Parenting: A Parent's Guide to Raising Happy and Successful Children, 4th Edition,* Videos (Active Parenting Publishers, 2014) video.

Preach My Gospel: A Guide to Missionary Service, "How Do I Develop Christ-like Attributes: Patience," Salt Lake City: Church of Jesus Christ of Latter-day Saints, 2018, 126.

Renlund, Dale G., "Choose You This Day," *Ensign,* November 2018.

Robbins, Lynn G., "Anger and Agency," *Ensign,* May 1998.

——, "Until Seventy Time Seven," *Ensign,* May 2018.

Scott, Richard G., "The Power of Correct Principles," *Ensign,* May 1993.

Stevens, Jean A., "Fear Not; I Am with Thee," *Ensign,* May 2014.

Utchdorf, Dieter F., "Continue in Patience," *Ensign,* May 2010.

Wirthlin, Joseph B., "The Virtue of Kindness," *Ensign,* April 2005.

Worthen, Kevin J., *Enduring Joy,* BYU Devotional, Jananuary 7, 2020. https://speeches.byu.edu/talks/kevin-j-worthen/enduring-joy

Young, K. Richard, *Kindness: A Celestial Touchstone,* BYU Address, November 1, 2005. https://speeches.byu.edu/talks/k-richard-young/kindness-celestial-touchstone/

——, *Relationship Bank,* Ward Fireside, given in Logan, Utah, November 13, 1994.

Acknowledgments

Oh, where to start . . . I will be forever grateful to Jesus Christ for His example, words, and atoning sacrifice. He truly makes and shows us the way in all things.

To my husband, Kerry, and our wonderful, growing crew. Life has been a grand adventure with all its ups and downs and twists and turns! I'm glad I get to be with all of you! Love you all bunches!

Thanks to my parents and siblings for giving me a soft place to land when I made mistakes and helping me have a childhood full of clean mountain air, love, laughter, and science experiments in our kitchen. Mom, you had to put up with a lot. Sorry about the red jello incident.

To Kirsten, Liz, Merilee, Bethany, and Kate for putting up with me and continuing to be my friends even when I blathered on about this project. To Chris Heiner for posing the question, "Would studying His attributes help us be better parents?" Your example inspired me to think deeply about important things.

Special thanks to Dr. Glenn Latham, Dr. Michael Popkin, and Dr. Richard Young for being the voices in my head that helped me find a better way to parent my children. Your research, insights, and love made all the difference to me. Thanks for finding a way to bless so many children's lives.

Andrea Smith, thanks for letting Jesus smile when He felt joy and creating such a wonderful image for the cover.

To my bookish friends Jeremy Madsen, KaTrina Jackson, the team at Eschler Editing, and the wonderful team at Cedar Fort! Your eyes were better than mine, and your kind encouragement kept me going. My heart is full, and my cup runneth over!

About the Author

Sherene Van Dyke is a wife, grandmother, and flawed mother of five who served her children tears for breakfast too often and so she turned to Jesus Christ with her parenting concerns. Twenty-five years later, she is still learning new things and helping others as she teaches parenting classes. Teaching these classes helped her connect the attributes of the Savior to good parenting practices. She has been a mother in seven states and three countries and loves spending time with family especially when conquering castles, hiking to waterfalls, or playing board games. Join Sherene for breakfast, lunch, or dinner to improve what you serve your family.

Visit christ-centered-parent.com
by scanning the QR code